THE GANDHIAN PHILOSOPHY
OF
THE SPINNING-WHEEL

GANDHIAN STUDIES AND PEACE RESEARCH SERIES

1. Gandhian Model of Development and World Peace / **R.P. Misra**
2. Conflict Resolution Through Non-Violence: Role of the Universities Volume I: Science and Ethics / **K.D. Gangrade** and **R.P. Misra**
3. Conflict Resolution Through Non-Violence: Role of Universities Volume II: Development Without Destruction / **K.D. Gangrade** and **R.P. Misra**
4. The Social Philosophy of Mahatma Gandhi / **K.S. Bharathi**
5. Gandhian Humanism / **Mohit Chakrabarty**
6. Gandhian Holistic Economics / **Shashi Prabha Sharma**
7. Gandhian Spiritualism: A Quest for the Essence of Excellence / **Mohit Chakrabarty**
8. Gandhian Perspective on Population and Development / **A.K. Sharma**
9. Thoughts of Gandhi and Vinoba : A Comparative Study / **K.S. Bharathi**
10. Economic Philosophy of Mahatma Gandhi / **Shanti Swarup Gupta**
11. Political Thoughts of Mahatma Gandhi / **K. S. Bharathi**
12. Gandhi and 21st Century / **Janardan Pandey** (Ed.)
13. Gandhian Philosophy of the Spinning-Wheel / **Mohit Chakrabarti**

About the Author

Mohit Chakrabarti (b. 1941) teaches Education and English at Visva-Bharati University, Santiniketan-731235, India. Frequently participates and presents papers in National/ International Conferences, Seminars, Symposia, Workshops etc. Significant participation/ presentation/acceptance of papers in the World Assembly of Teacher-Educators, the university of the West Indies, Kingston, Jamaica, Beijing Normal University, Beijing, People's Republic of China; The Institute of Education, Republic of Singapore, The University of Haifa, Israel.

Translator, book-reviewer, poet and critic, profusely writes in many periodicals and research journals of repute.

Writer of children's books in English and Bengali. Honoured with National Award as teacher educator. Credited with publications on literature, education and philosophy of Mahatma Gandhi, Rabindranath Tagore and Swami Vivekananda.

Recently awarded the D. Litt Degree by Visva-Bharati University.

Gandhian Studies and Peace Research Series—13

THE GANDHIAN PHILOSOPHY OF THE SPINNING-WHEEL

MOHIT CHAKRABARTI
Professor of Education
Visva-Bharati University
Santiniketan, West Bengal

CONCEPT PUBLISHING COMPANY, NEW DELHI - 110059

ISBN 81-7022-787-9

First Published 2000

Published and Printed by
Ashok Kumar Mittal
Concept Publishing Company
A/15-16, Commercial Block, Mohan Garden,
NEW DELHI - 110059 (India)

Phone: 5648039, 5649024
Fax : 091-(11)-5648053

Dedicated to
Dr. Mahendra Kumar
Editor, 'Gandhi Marg'
Gandhi Peace Foundation
New Delhi

Professor Dilip Kumar Sinha
Vice-Chancellor
Visva-Bharati University
Santiniketan

PREFACE

For the first time and perhaps for eternity the spinning-wheel as introduced by Mahatma Gandhi serves as the most serene and potent force for acceleration and emancipation of mankind. It acts as the mirror of the mind–the mirror that upholds the true image of man who knows no defeat in this untiring and undaunted endeavour for ascent and excellence. It reflects the spirit unending–the spirit that shows the advancement of erudition and edification of mankind. It also reflects man in terms of society—global or otherwise—and vice versa, thus enabling him to crystallize and recrystallize the errors and pitfalls in day-to-day dry thoughts and experiments, actions and contemplations.

The aims and objectives of the spinning-wheel as Gandhi spells out in his philosophy of work as worship encompasses the spirit of self-dependence both inwardly and outwardly. As an inward spirit, the spinning-wheel as he introspects, epitomises man, the Divine Being. As an outward spirit, it emphasizes on self-help, self-service, self-contentment and austerity. At the same time, the religion of the labour of love and identification with simplicity, modesty, sympathy and oneness as inherent in the spinning-wheel find an incomparable exposure in Gandhi's silent but steadfast dissemination of the soul-force.

That true education is always self-purification for better and greater devotion to unfold the True, Good and Beautiful deserves a genuine and ceaseless endeavour to bring about a happy unison between work and education. That is why Gandhi introduces the *Nai Talim* where the spinning-wheel plays a very significant role. "Education and the Spinning-wheel: Gandhian Perspectives" is a study in detail towards spelling out this essential objective.

Gandhi makes inroads to social awareness by means of introducing the spinning-wheel. It serves the three-fold purpose of making the right use of time and energy, arresting idleness and other social ills and stimulating the true social spirit of co-operation and harmony in one and all. With introduction of the spinning-wheel Gandhi never claims to be a social revolutionary as one would normally do, nor does he ever aspire after being recalled as a so-called social synchroniser, but deep in his heart of hearts quite unparalleled in the history of human progress and civilization, he believes in, and translates into reality, the spirit of self-discipline which can very well be cultivated and disseminated amongst all by an unambiguous and genuine involvement in the spinning-wheel. "Society and the Spinning-wheel: Gandhian Inroads" is a modest pointer to this direction.

Very often misunderstood and misinterpreted, the Gandhian philosophy of non-violence remains appallingly alienated from the Gandhian Philosophy of the spinning-wheel. As a matter of fact, the spinning-wheel and non-violence are so closely interlinked that in the absence of the one, the other becomes ambiguous and, let as frankly admit, meaningless. The points of unison between the two are legion. Both represents the truth-force and the soul-force. Both steer one towards self-emancipation and self-ascent. Both boost one in quest of excellence beyond excellence. "Non-violence and the Spinning-wheel: Gandhian Points of Unison" is an humble endeavour to probe these and other points of unison.

Gandhian religion represents the religion of man as the embodiment of All Serene. Gandhi visualizes man the Divine Being—*Naranarayan*—in the poor representing the same Divine Being—*Daridranarayan*. How does he introspect so? What prompts him to launch a crusade against poverty by means of the spinning-wheel in order to highlight it as a matchless vehicle to encounter the All Beautiful in the poor and the down-trodden? "Religion and the Spinning-Wheel: Gandhian Introspection" may ensure Gandhian religion and the spinning-wheel in the light of a newer angle of vision.

"Humanism and the Spinning-wheel: Gandhian Forethoughts" may evoke fresh thoughts and thrilling reactions among all interested in advancement of humanism.

I cannot but recall the profound scholarship of Dr. Mahendra Kumar, Editor, *Gandhi Marg*, Gandhi Peace Foundation, New Delhi and love and affection of Professor Dilip Kumar Sinha, Vice-Chancellor, Visva-Bharati University, Santiniketan-731235, West Bengal, who have inspired me in completing this work. I dedicate the book to them as an humble token of my gratitude.

If the book freely and spontaneously brings forth a genuine efflorescence of devotion to explore newer avenues of Gandhiana and serves as an undaunted challenge for overcoming the overzealous cybernetic mindset, I would feel myself prized with pompous premia.

MOHIT CHAKRABARTI

Seemantika
Seemanto Palli
Santiniketan-731235
West Bengal (India)

CONTENTS

1

AIMS AND OBJECTIVES OF THE SPINNING-WHEEL
Gandhian Viewpoints

MAHATMA GANDHI makes a global revolution by introducing the spinning-wheel amongst mankind in all walks of life. He assures everyone devoted to the spinning-wheel of ascent and excellence with which his divine being is identified and manifested when well-backed by the spirit of work as worship. Besides this divine component of work associated with devotion to the spinning-wheel as Gandhi always upholds, there is also an inherent truth that always guides humanity. This may be termed as an inward discipline in every human being. Just as a natural form of discipline is always prevalent, be it in the case of Nature and day-to-day happenings, so everyone cannot but admit the tremendous powerful discipline within himself even by remaining irresponsive at times notwithstanding. Hence, orientation and recycling of the self through exercise of discipline to be well-maintained by the spinning-wheel.

Why does Gandhi take recourse to the spinning-wheel when discipline is essentially a training of the mind which can be well-exercised by means of other media of exercise of the mind? The answer, as Gandhi advocates, is quite simple and clear. He is quite aware of the two types of discipline necessary for the growth and development of being viz., inward and outward. Quite unlike other humanists, Gandhi launches his programme for introducing the spinning-wheel to serve the twin purposes of inward discipline while undergoing outer discipline or discipline in the extrinsic form at the same time.

Again, Gandhi introduces the spinning-wheel as the only easiest alternative for the masses to utilize time in the best possible way for the benefit of the individual as well as of the society. The dream of the spinning-wheel as he visualizes is the dream for better emancipation of man as an individual and social being. In his aims and objectives of introducing the spinning-wheel Gandhi encapsulates the following parameters:

(a) To revitalize the socio-economic status of an individual in right earnest by catering to the immediate needs and intentions for a desirable growth and development of the individual and the society.
(b) To stimulate the individual to earnestly respond to the truth that work is worship.
(c) To provide an atmosphere of awareness to the self so that exercise of the innovative spirit of man is made during leisure period.
(d) To bring about a positive change in social inconsistencies as revealed in diverse stratification of the society where the self-esteem of an individual suffers from absence of awareness and exercise of inner sensibilities.
(e) To accelerate the spirit of self-dependence and self-help so that everyone in the society is inspired with the dynamic role for conforming strictly to work-ethics and work-culture.
(f) To encourage everyone in the society to be responsive to individual and social emancipation by a practical approach to self-realization and self-dignity.
(g) To inspire everyone to be true to his divine being so that the spirit of divinity embodied in every individual in the society is well apprehended in course of exercise of the deeper social problems of life.
(h) To awaken a sense of practical humanism where involvement of the self by means of self service makes a steadier course of unison with the true spirit of humanism.
(i) To cultivate a certain sense of beyonding of man and society by means of ascent and excellence of the nobler spirits of mankind.
(j) To equip the individual to be above all kinds of narrowness and partisan spirit and embrace all men and society in the purest and most perfect vision of global men and global society. This will certainly be a positive response to the most cherished aim of *Vasudhaiva-Kutumvakam*—embracing the world as the most endearing abode of mankind.

Admittedly, in framing and conceptualizing the aims and objectives of the spinning-wheel, Gandhi does not intend to launch any rigorous principle and theory but adores and exposes simplicity in day-to-day response to work as worship for better efflorescence of man and society. As he categorically remarks.

> If I preach against the modern artificial life of sensual enjoyment, and ask men and women to go back to the simple life epitomized in the *Charkha* I do so because I know that without an intelligent return to simplicity, there is no escape from our descent to a state lower than brutality.
>
> — M.K. Gandhi: *Harijan,* 8 May 1937.

To make 'an intelligent return to simplicity' by associating oneself sincerely to the spinning-wheel is to consolidate one's position in self-dignity and self-reliance. In fact, Gandhi goes so far as to spell out the aims and objectives of the spinning-wheel in terms of comparing it to the Sun which is the most powerful source of energy and light and assuring it of its supreme position among all kinds of handicrafts. On February 10, 1938, while delivering his speech on the occasion of opening of the All-India Village Industries and Khadi Exhibition, Gandhi has referred to purity of life which can be well attained by means of involvement in the programme of activities related to the spinning-wheel and his vision of the spinning wheel is later on exposed in Haripura as follows:

> I have often said that if seven lakhs of the villages of India were to be kept alive, and if peace that is at the root of civilization is to be achieved, we have to make the spinning-wheel the centre of all handicrafts. Thus my faith in the spinning-wheel is growing every-day and I see it more and more clearly that the Sun of the wheel will alone illumine the planets of other handicrafts. But I go further and say that just as we go on discovering the new stars and planets in the vast solar system, even so we should go on discovering fresh handicrafts everyday. But for the sake of this thing we shall have to make the spinning-wheel the really life-giving Sun.
>
> — D.G. Tendulkar, *Mahatma,* Publications Division, Ministry of Information and Broadcasting, Government of India, 1969, Vol. IV, pp. 215-216.

To liberate mankind from physical, mental and spiritual death, Gandhi highlights the spinning-wheel, and in so doing, he refers to the indomitable spirit of man that never yields to any force—internal or external—whatsoever. He believes in the force of self-denial where, too, the spinning-wheel serves as a very positive force to do away with artificiality, luxury, affluence and passivity and welcome simplicity, austerity, truth and living and thrilling involvement in life and society. In fact, the primary objective of introducing the spinning-wheel as Gandhi incorporates, is to accept all challenges of life that appear in the forms of greed, mechanomania, passivity and indolence in particular and wage a crusade against all these temptations and undesirable circumstances standing in the way of the progressive march of mankind and efflorescence of inwardness of vision.

To channelize the spirit of inwardness by introducing the spinning-wheel among people in every society, Gandhi visualizes the fourfold approach to emancipation of the self which may be analysed as follows:

(a) *Equality of Man*

According to this approach, the essential component of mutual respect to be retained and accelerated with all care and caution is indirectly exercised through the spinning-wheel. A fine thread of unison is exquisitely woven in course of sharing the woes of the poor and the distressed, where the inward vision of embracing everyone as one's eternal friend or neighbour is well-enkindled in the blessings of purity. Hence, the importance of introducing the spinning-wheel to sufficiently explore and inspire the justified vision of equality of man from the point of excellence and qualitative emancipation.

Moreover, Gandhi also points our attention towards the direction of the desirable ascent of man, where the spinning-wheel serves as the basic synchronizer of humane sensibilities. The seedlings of selflessness and altruism are thus indirectly nurtured and protected by the spinning-wheel.

(b) *Exercise of Austerity*

To mould life and society in the pattern of simplicity and austerity is very essential for human progress and human civilization. Gandhi directs our attention towards exercise of simplicity and austerity by means of exercise of the spinning-wheel primarily because the latter makes a bond between theory and practice in work as worship and minimizes wastage of time and energy. Moreover, as it entails less care and caution at the time of operation and involves a very little amount of money it welcomes the participation of one and all in the form of a joyous endeavour and pulsating adventure to lead a life of simplicity and austerity. This also suggests a veritable promise in bringing about an effective change in life and society.

(c) *Exercise of Aesthetic Sensibilities*

Unlike other humanitarians and social thinkers, Gandhi wages a war against, erosion of aesthetic sensibilities in the day-to-day life of man in society. An appalling absence of exercise of Beauty, Goodness and Truth in every kind of work has terribly pained him. Moreover, the superiority of mechanism and passivity so disastrously engulfing the inner man in an overabundance of gadgets and softwares has rightly and alarmingly posed an extinction of finer sensibilities and aesthetic visions of man. Gandhi's principal concern is to bring back the essence of aesthetics specially in relation to the inherent qualities of Goodness, Beauty and Truth in life and society by means of introducing the spinning-wheel in every home. A certain sense of restraint in behaviour so well exercised by involvement in such an instrument of orientation in personal and social life also indicates the fact that the special role of the spinning-wheel is to allow people in all stratas of the society to cultivate ease and grace consciously and effectively.

(d) *Exercise of Spirituality*

Perhaps the most significant objective of the spinning-wheel as Gandhi considers in advocating it is to exercise the inherent spirituality in every human being. Herein lies the intrinsic role of the spinning-wheel in moulding the minds of the masses towards excellence and ascent. Gandhi's primary intention of involvement of man in the spinning-wheel is thus a strong indication to the fact that he not only considers it a mere tool for utilizing leisure hours but also a very effective means of looking inwardly and looking within for poignance and serenity so essential to the fulness of vision and development of personality so estranged in the absence of 'austere civilisation.'[1]

The vision with which Gandhi enriches his philosophy of the spinning-wheel is to identify the All Serene amidst communal and social harmony well brought forth in course of the exercise of the spinning-wheel. This is why he earnestly deserves that the sanctity of the spinning-wheel as a bridge between man and his divine being must be maintained at any cost. This is undeniably a new concept of spirituality which is dynamic and practical in its essence of exposition in its purest form. As he significantly asserts.

> My God is myriad-formed and while sometimes I see Him in the spinning-wheel, at other times I see Him in the communal unity, then again in the removal of untouchability, and that is how I establish communion with Him according as the spirit moves me.
>
> — M.K. Gandhi, *Harijan,* 8 May, 1937.

Reorientation of education by means of introducing the spinning-wheel in the programmes of education for children in particular as Gandhi has designed in Basic Education is, indeed, a silent revolution for regeneration of consciousness. This not only shows a positive step towards restoration of self-reliance and self-help but also to avert the tragedy of wastage in money, manpower and materials as we even now come across in our oversimplified, mechanical, passive and computerized life. As a practical educationist, he wants education to be a vital source of human efflorescence of consciousness and this is why he deliberately points out of his own experiences the glaring differences of opportunities between the villages and the towns in education and growth. The nursling of complexes manifold and diverse in between these two has forced the power of alienation to thrive in a favourable atmosphere of hatred and ignorance, passivity and arrogance. Gandhi wants to uproot this evil force by introducing the spinning-wheel as a vocational course of education for children of both rural and urban areas. His suggestions in this connection are very distinct.

> What kinds of vocations are the fittest for being taught to children in urban schools? There is no hard and fast rule about it. But my reply is clear. I want to resuscitate the villages of India. Today our villages have become a mere appendage to the cities. They exist, as it were, to be exploited by the latter and depend on the latter's sufferance. This is unnatural. It is only when the cities realize the duty of making an adequate return to the villages for the strength and sustenance which they derive from them, instead of selfishly exploiting them, that a healthy and moral relationship between the two will spring up. And if the city children are to play their part in this great and noble work of social reconstruction, the vocations through which they are to achieve their education ought to be directly related to the requirements of the villages. So far as I can see, the various processes of cotton manufacture from ginning and cleaning of cotton to the spinning of yarn, answer this test as

> nothing else does. Even today cotton is grown in the villages and is ginned and spun and converted into cloth in the cities. But the chain of processes which cotton undergoes in the mills from the beginning to the end constitutes a huge tragedy of waste in men, materials and mechanical power.
>
> — M.K. Gandhi, *Harijan,* 9 October, 1937.

Admittedly, education for social consciousness and national integration earnestly awaits the role of the spinning-wheel. To utilize the spinning-wheel as the bond of love, sympathy, mutual understanding and co-operation among the masses and at the same time save the country from 'economic drain' as Gandhi categorically asserts is one of the most significant aims and objectives which he also wants to emphasize on the education of children right from their school stage. His main concern is all-round awareness to social and national disparities to be brought about by means of introducing the spinning-wheel and equip the learners to accept the challenges of exploitation. Reacting strongly to a student's remark that spinning is merely a wastage of time and energy and it does not negotiate the principle of division of labour, Gandhi characteristically elucidates the aims and objectives of the spinning-wheel in terms of the above and dispels all confusion and misconception related to it.

> Do I ask you to do spinning for the whole day? Do I ask you to take it up as a substantive occupation? Where, then, is the breach of the principle of division of labour? Do you have a division of labour in eating and drinking? Just as everyone of us must eat and drink and clothe himself, even so everyone of us must spin himself. And it is a waste, you say? Fellow-feeling for your countrymen, you say, you have in an abundant measure? And what is that fellow-feeling, without the milk of human kindness? Do you feel anything like the love that a cow feels for her calf or a mother for her baby? The cow's udders and the mother's breast overflow with milk at the sight of their young ones. Do your hearts overflow with love at the sight of your famished countrymen? By spinning, my friends, you demonstrate your love for them. You spin and you make them shake off their idleness. A friend goes and beautifully sings before a crowd and affects their hearts. Is it a waste of effort? It would be, of course, if he vainly howls 'Bande Mataram' before them. But spinning means more. It has purpose and it means added production. The purpose is that it serves as a bond with the

> masses. And the mechanical effort has something as its result whilst there is absolutely nothing like spinning which all alike can do without much effort and skill, nothing which can be done by millions, by the best of us, as by the mediocre. And the students should all do it particularly because they are the salt of the earth. Their life is yet to begin, they can imbibe new ideas as no one else can; and they have years of service before them. You will perhaps think of England with her elaborate machinery. But she lives on the exploitation of other nations. It is an economic drain which is even more disastrous than the home charges and other drains that Dadabhai Naoroji opened our eyes to. Even he could not see this insidious drain, but I being his disciple, working along his lines, have discovered this subtle drain and say that economic drain involved in our being made a nation of idlers is the most ruinous of all.
>
> —D.G. Tendulkar: *Mahatma,* Publications Division, Ministry of Information and Broadcasting, Government of India, 1969, Vol. II, pp. 185-86.

Undeniably, to remove economic disparity and starvation to a positive extent from the society, Gandhi accelerates on the spinning movement. He directs everyone's attention towards an all-round vigil for wants, aspirations and deficiencies of the spinners and a new sense of optimism to bring forth a ray of better standard of living among the poor and distressed people in the society. He also warns against the role of the middlemen who are always alert in grabbing the lion's share and deprive the spinners to eke out through supplementary employment. As a practical observer of the spinning movement, he spells out the aims and objectives in terms of its vital, permanent and effective dissemination and the safety of the spinners from hopelessness and frustration. From January 11 to January 19, 1927, Gandhi makes an extensive tour in Bihar and on January 20, 1927 he exposes the true picture of the effectiveness of the spinning-wheel, wherein he also spells out in *Young India* its objectives as follows:

> During my tour, in so far as it has progressed up to now, I have observed that the spinning organizations have not an accurate register of the spinners and that the figures supplied and published by me from time to time in these pages were based upon the deductions drawn from the actual wages paid to the spinners. For statistical information, the calculation is sound enough, because it

must err on the right side, that is, of understatement. But it is not good enough for the movement itself. The spinning movement depends for its permanence upon a vital and direct contact being established between the workers and the spinners; for, then only shall we be able to understand the wants and aspirations and limitations of the spinners. The object is to penetrate the remotest homes in the innumerable villages of India and to introduce a ray of hope and light into these homes. And this we shall never do, if we do not establish a living touch with the spinners. We cannot, therefore, be satisfied with the work of middlemen whom we may not and do not know. We must be able to trace the course of every pie until it is safely deposited in the hands of the spinners. Let it be remembered that spinning is the central fact of the movement, not weaving, not dyeing, not printing, not even carding and ginning, anterior though the last two processes are to spinning. For, the economic solution depends upon a supplementary employment being found for the largest number of the semi-starved millions. That employment by far the best is spinning and that alone.

— M.K. Gandhi, *Young India,* 20 January, 1927.

Gandhi's inward vision with regard to the introduction of the spinning for a better regeneration of India has its relevance even now. Right from the vision of affluence with liberal economy and industrial policy, the spinning-wheel has its inherent appeal to the finer and softer sensibilities whereby the aesthetic appeal of mankind may be well-balanced with the desirable restraint and discipline of mind. As a foreseer and humanist *par excellence.* Gandhi always reminds us of the fact that unless man is in a position to control his greed for luxury materialistic or whatsoever by means of undergoing an effective programme of discipline that cares for altruism, he cannot but encounter extinction in no time. A balanced economy as one would appreciate, also encompasses a balanced approach to life and society. Gandhi harps on the spinning-wheel to harmonize humanity with this balanced approach to life and society. This end-in-view of the spinning-wheel remarkably rewards man with two very worthy dividends: humility and self-respect. In case of humility which is one of the most important component of enriched personality, Gandhi always reminds us of the very positive role of the spinning-wheel where purity and sincerity in our endeavour or involvement are to be maintained with all care and caution. The point of self-respect to be maintained at all cost in order to be justified to humanism is all the more important because it indicates man's devotion to both inward and outward excellence. Referring to the two aspects—'terrible and benign'—to bring about *Swaraj* and to infuse new life and hope to the hapless villagers by means of the spinning-wheel, Gandhi appeals on the eve of the All India Congress Committee Meeting, 1927 at Ahmedabad.

> I believe in *Khaddar,* I believe in the spinning-wheel. It has two aspects, terrible and benign. In its terrible aspect it is calculated to bring about the only boycott we need for independent national existence, viz., that of the foreign cloth. It alone can kill the demoralizing British self-interest. In its benign aspect it gives a new life and hope to the villager. It can fill millions of hungry mouths. It alone can bring us in touch and in tune with the villagers. It is the very best popular education that is needed for the millions. It is life-giving. I would not hesitate in the least to turn the Congress into an exclusively *Khaddar*-producing and *Khaddar* propaganda organization till the attainment of *Swaraj,* just as I would not hesitate, if I believed in the use of arms and giving violent battle to England, to make the Congress an organization exclusively devoted to training the nation in the use of arms. To be truly national the Congress must devote itself exclusively to that which will bring the nation most quickly within reach of *Swaraj.* Because I believe in the potency of *Khaddar* to give *Swaraj.* I have given it the foremost place in our programme.
>
> — D.G. Tendulkar: *Mahatma,* Publications Division, Ministry of Information and Broadcasting, Government of India, 1969, Vol. II, pp. 137-138.

Gandhi is also interested in the multi-embracing aims and objectives of the spinning-wheel and all these as he firmly advocates, would certainly bring about remarkable revolution in national and social awareness. As he categorically points out:

> Round the *Charkha,* that is, amidst the people who have shed their idleness and who have understood the value of co-operation, a national servant would build up a programme of anti-malaria campaign, improved sanitation, settlement of the village disputes, conservation and breeding of cattle and hundreds of other beneficial activities. Wherever the *Charkha* work is fairly established, all such ameliorative activity is going on according to the capacity of the villagers and the workers concerned.
>
> — *Ibid.,* p. 217.

Never a 'dying cult' but a perennial living inspiration, the spinning-wheel as Gandhi strongly advocates, is a continual inspirer in exercising self-esteem and self-sacrifice. It enriches and never belittles the soul of man. 'There is no fall in the barometer of *Khaddar'*, as his long-standing experience prompts him to assure mankind. A passport to the hearts of the *hoi polloi,* it promises a new generation who will forsake vainglory and complex of the so-called civilization where the ascent and excellence of the inward man are relegated to the background.

An unparalleled avenue of mass awareness as the spinning-wheel ably contains within itself, the modern world always remains indebted to the incomparable spirit of emancipation of man which Gandhi brings forth in the launching of the spinning-wheel, not merely as an instrument of extrinsic change, but also a serene vehicle of communion with the All Beautiful. As he frankly observes:

> I do not know whether I am a *Karmayogi* or any other *Yogi.* I know that I cannot live without work. I crave to die with my hand at the spinning-wheel. If one has to establish communion with God through some means, why not through the spinning-wheel?
>
> — M.K. Gandhi: *Harijan,* 8 May, 1937.

Who else than Mahatma Gandhi can elevate humanism to be in unison with divinity?

NOTE

1. Maurice Frydman, a celebrated Polish-born engineer and close associate of Mahatma Gandhi reveals how Gandhi evaluates man in terms of the spiritual and the aesthetic ends-in-view of the spinning-wheel:
'Therefore I want simple machines, not big monsters which nobody can possess.' He (Gandhi) said, 'My ideal is a machine which anybody can have.' I personally feel that man comes first, and he also used to say: With me man comes first. 'What is good for man is good for Gandhiji; what is not good for man is not good for Gandhiji.' But the difficulty arises in judgement, in the judgement what is good. A certain amount of well-being is good—beyond that it comes altogether bad. To know where to stop, to stick to the medium—to the middle way—is wisdom to him. We may consider that his standard of life which he considered sufficient, is too low for us, but he takes the ascetic attitude. Hindu as he is, and bread alone, as far as material goods are concerned, is enough for him. He does not need anything more. So a little food, some clothing, a modest shelter is all that he asks for man, for his material being; the rest he leaves alone. The civilisation built on his principles would be a very austere civilisation.
— Francis Watson & Maurice Brown: *Talking of Gandhiji,* Orient Longmans, Calcutta, 1957, pp. 44-45.

2

EDUCATION AND THE SPINNING-WHEEL
Gandhian Perspectives

EDUCATION is always a process of continual emancipation. It is a process of looking within oneself. To Mahatma Gandhi, education is more than mere emancipation or bare looking within oneself. It is emancipation of the divine being within oneself and a silent but certain process of the beyonding of man. It is a dynamic, living, exploring and re-exploring exercise of the being of oneself which encompasses the entire global spectrum of a global society of inter-dependent and conjoint endeavour at the ascent and excellence of man.

How does Gandhi allow mankind to explore and re-explore for the end-in-view of education as above? What prompts him to nursle the seeds of humanism and socio-aesthetics in education? Obviously, the introduction of the spinning-wheel to exercise the power of the enkindling of the self for the emancipation of the divine self within everyone is an unparalleled adventure which he keeps wide open to be allowed to beckon and to be undertaken by the elusive humanity. As a matter of fact, his radical approach to Basic Education incorporates the spinning-wheel as one of the most characteristic means of exercise of the spirit of self-esteem, self-dependence and self-analysis which abundantly contribute to the efflorescence of aesthetics and exercise of the positive spirit of humanism in a global society of interdependence and advancement of finer sensibilities and softer visions of life. Elucidating the immense educational value of the spinning-wheel to the students, Gandhi asserts:

> A cause is often greater than man. Certainly the spinning-wheel is greater than myself. With it, in my opinion, is mixed up the well-being of the whole mass of Indian humanity. The pupils should,

> therefore, learn something about the deep poverty of the masses. They should have an ocular demonstration of some villages that are crumbling down to pieces. They should know the population of India. They should know the vast extent of this peninsula and they should know what it is that all the millions can do to add to their scanty resources. They should learn to identify themselves with the poor and the downtrodden in the land. They should be taught to deny themselves, so far as possible, the things that the poorest cannot have. Then they will understand the virtue of hand-spinning. It will then survive any shock including disillusionment about myself. The cuase of the spinning-wheel is too great and too good to have to rest on mere hero-worship. It lends itself to scientific economic treatment.
>
> — D.G. Tendulkar: *Mahatma,* Publications Division, Ministry of Information and Broadcasting, Government of India, 1969, Vol. II, pp. 228-29.

Deeply concerned with the education of children, Gandhi wants to introduce the spinning-wheel which will, as he strongly believes and experiments in his own school, harmonize his body, mind and soul. The education he receives must not be allowed to make him crippled and atrophied. The education for emancipation of the child's mind and spirit, body and soul can be smoothly and effectively imparted through an exercise of the spinning-wheel that teaches the lesson of work as worship. His own words with regard to the education of the child from this end-in-view express the point better.

> I would develop in the child his hands, his brain and his soul. The hands have almost atrophied. The soul has been altogether ignored.
>
> — R.K. Prabhu & U.R. Rao (compiled): *The Mind of Mahatma Gandhi,* Oxford University Press, London, 1945, p. 161.

Gandhi of course, expands the horizon of education through the spinning-wheel by extending its role in rural regeneration. In fact, he wants to equip students to convey the message of the spinning-wheel in every village. During major vacations in the schools they will participate in the programmes of dissemination of the spinning-wheel among people specially in villages to make them self-reliant and self-conscious. Moreover, this will also bring about a radical change in rural economy. The students will, indeed, be amply enriched with the down-to-earth experiences of rural life with all its appalling poverty, ignorance, superstition, injustice etc. and share the common lot of man with a definite promise of change by means of launching the spinning-wheel. Gandhi's appeal to the students of the Gujarat Vidyapith elucidates his vision of the spinning-wheel as follows:

> We know only through history the condition of the villages, not within easy reach of the railway stations. The only loving tie of service that can bind the villages to us is the spinning-wheel. Those who have not understood this are in this institution to no purpose. The education is not 'national' that takes no account of the starving millions of India and that devises no means for their relief. Government contact with the villages ends with the collection of revenue. Our contact with them begins with their service through the spinning-wheel, but it does not end there. The spinning-wheel is the centre of that service. If you spend your next vacation in some far off village in the interior, you will find the people cheerless and fear-stricken. You will find the houses in ruins. And you will look in vain for any sanitary and hygienic conditions. You will find the cattle in a miserable way, and you will see idleness stalking there. The people will tell you of the spinning-wheel having been in their homes long ago, but today they will entertain no talk of it or any other cottage industry. They have no hope left in them. They live, for they cannot die at will. They will spin only if you spin.
>
> —D.G. Tendulkar: *Mahatma* Publications Division, Ministry of Information and Broadcasting, Government of India, 1969, Vol. II, p. 229.

With changed national perspectives of rural development and rural economy since independence, the country is yet to ameliorate the distress and woes of the rural people in particular. Even education with all its nobler aims and greater objectives to minimize the differences between the rich and the poor, the high and the low, the advantaged and the disadvantaged has failed to bridge the ever widening gap between the rural and the urban people. This has been further aggravated when in the name of national integration and social awareness programmes like educational excursions, social camps etc. are organised in villages or towns where a peculiar atmosphere of undesirable complex thrives in a rampant manner. Thanks to computer-crazy modernity, the rural people, too, rush for automation without caring for its viability in the Indian context of man-power and economy, education and indispensable resources leaving aside indigenous avenues of enrichment of body and mind by means of the spinning-wheel. In fact, the spinning-wheel which can even now make a thrilling revolution in boosting national morale and national advancement specially in restoring and enriching purity of character and a strong sense of love for one and all in every nook and corner of the country has been relegated to oblivion. Today's learners simply wonder at the extraordinary power of the spinning-wheel in bringing the entire nation in a cordial platform of oneness and unity, sympathy and fraternity.

Admittedly, it is high time to recall Gandhi's invaluable words to revive 'purity of character in action' through the spinning-wheel as one of the most essential objectives of education.

> If you will express the requisite purity of character in action, you cannot do it better than through the spinning-wheel. Of all the myriads of God, *Daridranarayan* is the most sacred, in as much as it represents the untold millions of the poor people as distinguished from the few rich people. The easiest and the best way of identifying yourselves somewhat with these starving millions is to spread the message of the spinning-wheel in the threefold manner suggested by me. You can spread it by becoming expert spinners, by wearing Khadi and by pecuniary contributions.
>
> —*Ibid.*, p. 377.

To make education self-reliant and self-supporting, the spinning-wheel can even now play a very significant role. If introduced at the primary level in school education in, of course, right earnest it will definitely pay worthy dividends in manifold ways as follows:

(i) It will bring forth among pupils a certain sense of national consciousness.
(ii) It will enable them to undergo manual training.
(iii) It will teach them how to make the right use of time.
(iv) It will encourage them to be disciplined in the true sense of the term.
(v) It will enable them to enrich their mental health along with physical exercise.
(vi) It will curb every possible mischievous tendency by means of maintenance of discipline.

Speaking at length on the economics of education which comprises the role of the spinning-wheel in harmonizing the various faculties of body, mind and soul, Gandhi advocates 'the education of the heart' for the 'making of the whole man' as follows.

> The baneful effects of absence of proper co-ordination and harmony among the various faculties of body, mind and soul respectively are obvious. They are all around us; only we have lost perception of them owing to their present perverse associations. Take the case of our village folk. From their childhood upward they toil and labour in their fields from morning till night like their cattle in the midst of whom they live. Their existence is a weary, endless round of mechanical drudgery unrelieved by a spark of intelligence or higher grace of life. Deprived of all scope for developing their mind and soul, they have sunk to the level of the beast. Life to them is a sorry bungle which they muddle through anyhow. On the other hand, what goes by the name of education in our schools and colleges in the cities today is in reality only intellectual dissipation. Intellectual training is there looked upon as something altogether unrelated to manual or physical work. But since the body must have some sort of physical exercise to keep it in health, they vainly try to attain that end by means of an artificial and otherwise barren system of physical culture which would be ridiculous beyond words if the result was not so tragic. The young man who emerges from this system can in no way compete in physical endurance with an ordinary labourer. The slightest physical exertion gives him headache; a mild exposure to the sun is enough to cause him giddiness. And what is more, all this is looked upon as quite 'natural'.
>
> * * * * *
>
> As against this, take the case of a child in whom the education of the heart is attended to from the very beginning. Supposing he is set to some useful occupation like spinning, carpentry, agriculture etc., for his education, and in that connection is given a thorough comprehensive knowledge relating to the theory of the various operations that he is to perform, and the use and construction of the tools, that he would be wielding. He would not only develop a fine, healthy body but also a sound, vigorous intellect that is not merely academic but is firmly rooted in and is tested from day-to-day experience. His intellectual education would include a

knowledge of mathematics and the various sciences that are useful for an intelligent and efficient exercise of his avocation. If to this is added literature by way of recreation, it would give him a perfect, well-balanced, all-round education in which the intellect, the body and the spirit have all full play and develop together into a natural, harmonious whole. Man is neither mere intellect nor the gross animal body, nor the heart or soul alone. A proper and harmonious combination of all the three is required for the making of the whole man and constitutes the true economics of education.

— M.K. Gandhi: *Harijan,* 8 May, 1937.

Looking upon the spinning-wheel as the basis of the education of the child, Gandhi upholds the theory of learning by doing. In fact, all learning *sans* activity turns into worthless nonsense so far as the making of the complete man is concerned. Gandhi's interest in introducing the spinning-wheel is the interest of striving for fulness of growth and personality, where the learner's self-involvement in self-understanding and self-appreciation plays the most significant and vital role. The education of the heart as he aims at through incorporation of spinning as a compulsory course in the programme of education opens out at least the four-fold avenue of efflorescence of the personality of every learner.

(i) With spinning a certain sense of social and national consciousness is very strongly exercised.
(ii) Spinning allows the learner to expose his creative and aesthetic power of thinking in practice of performance.
(iii) The spinning-wheel brings forth the message of simplicity and austerity.
(iv) The spinning-wheel teaches the lesson of fellow-feeling and sharing the experiences of sorrows and sufferings of the poor and deprived humanity.

When Gandhi speaks of national education he emphasizes on introduction of the spinning-wheel in school education because the four-fold avenue of manifestation of pupil-personality necessitates an earnest approach to be exercised in full swing. His own definition of 'national education' elucidates the role of the spinning-wheel in education best:

That education is national which educates in you a sense of fellow-feeling for all your countrymen, which teaches you to melt at the

> woes of your countrymen. And nothing is so universally useful as the spinning-wheel.
>
> — D.G. Tendulkar: *Mahatma,* Publications Division, Ministry of Information and Broadcasting, Government of India, 1969, Vol. II, p. 185.

That the spinning-wheel is a science in itself and should be taken up a subject for study in every school to infuse the true spirit of nationalism amongst pupils are the facts still remaining unwarranted in the context of national identity and national development. An important lever of service for self-development, it has an unending power to overshadow any parallel competition simply by exercising the inherent will-force with which everyone is enriched. This is why he reminds the teachers of the place of the spinning-wheel in the syllabus of school education.

> The *Charkha* has a place on your programme, but it is one out of the four or five things you teach here. Now I want you to understand that the *Charkha* has a place all its own. For the reasons that should be obvious to you. For the *Charkha*—is not one of the professions that you teach. A profession is for earning a livelihood, and if the *Charkha* was to be taught as a profession, it should have no place in your syllabus. It has a special purpose. When you put it in a line with carpentry, clay-modelling and painting, you are guilty of a confusion of thought. *Charkha* is an instrument of service. In a national school, where the nation expects us to train national servants, the scheme of studies will centre round the *Charkha.* It is a science in itself and it is a science which gives us a knowledge of the means of ameliorating the condition of the masses. Do you know that we have not one national institution where mechanical engineering is taught and where good spindles are made? If you learn mechanics, concentrate on learning how to make a true spindle and how to mend a wrong one. You should be able to say the circumference of an ideal wheel, the distance between the axle and the poles, the number of revolutions of your spindle, etc. A carpenter in a national school will not have as his ambition the making of an ideal cabinet, but of an ideal *Charkha.* In short, you should study the *Charkha* scientifically and with religious zeal, with a view of making it the mightiest lever of the nation's salvation.
>
> — *Ibid.,* p. 253.

What Gandhi speaks on the educational aims and objectives of the spinning-wheel far back in 1927 to the teachers of the Khamgaon National School, Madhya Pradesh, has its relevance even now in the context of ample opportunities for studies in mechanical and other branches of engineering in the post-independent India. The fact that the education of the spinning-wheel is the education of self-esteem to be as one should be is the lesson yet to be learnt in the changed national perspectives.

To impart 'whole education', as Gandhi suggests, the practical training of students in the whole art and science of the spinning-wheel is of paramount importance. Crafts should not be introduced for the sake of crafts alone. In that case, these would lose the benefits of the essentials of learning that are beyond those of liberal education. To synchronize the practical training of the spinning-wheel with intellectual development makes education all the more thrilling and interesting. How to impart education of the spinning-wheel? What factors should be borne in mind when a teacher is engaged with the teaching of the spinning-wheel? Gandhi's own experience in this connection is noteworthy:

> I want that the whole education should be imparted through some handicrafts or industry. It might be objected that in the Middle Ages only handicrafts were taught to the students; but the occupational training, then, was far from serving an educational purpose. The crafts were taught only for the sake of the crafts, without any attempt to develop the intellect as well. In this age those born to certain professions had forgotten them, had taken to clerical careers, and were lost to the countryside. As a result, it is now impossible to find an efficient carpenter or smith in an average village. The handicrafts were nearly lost and the spinning-wheel being neglected was taken to Lancashire where it was developed, thanks to the English genius, to an extent that is seen today. This, I say, irrespective of my views on industrialism.
>
> The remedy lies in imparting the whole art and science of a craft through practical training and there through imparting the whole education. Teaching of *takli*-spinning, for instance, presupposes the imparting of knowledge of the various varieties of cotton, different soils in different provinces of India, the history of the ruin of the handicraft, its political reasons, which will include the history of the British rule in India, knowledge of arithmetic and so on. I am now trying the same experiment on my little grandson, who scarcely feels that he is being taught, for he all the while plays and laughs and sings. I am especially mentioning the

takli and emphasizing its utility, because I have realized its power and its romance, also because the handicraft of making cloth is the only one which can be taught throughout the country and because the *takli* is cheap. If you have any other suitable handicraft to suggest, please do so without hesitation, so that we might consider it as well. I am convinced that *takli* is the only practical solution of our problem, considering the deplorable economic condition now prevailing in the country.

— D.G. Tendulkar, *Mahatma,* Publications Division, Ministry of Information and Broadcasting, Government of India, 1969, Vol. IV, p. 191-92.

What Gandhi suggests as above in the historic Educational Conference at Wardha on October 22, 1937 deserves sincere attention even under colossal economic change in the post-independence era in our country. Today's education specially at the primary stage should incorporate spinning as an essential craft primarily because it even now contributes a lot to develop the power of introspection and self-esteem to every child at this stage. Moreover, an involvement in the spinning-wheel is now only educative but also exceedingly enjoyable because it allows each learner to have an easy and free access to the aesthetic world of Beauty, Truth and Goodness.

With the spinning-wheel the child-learner is perhaps best initiated into the world of the essentials of learning. For, the learner does not entangle or fall in the line with passive, mechanical, dull, disinterested and lifeless learning normally an unavoidable or compulsory factor often accompanied by cramming or rot learning. While spinning is a means of involvement in a dynamic activity, the psychological end-in-view of education in the form of learning by doing best synchronizes education with work and *vice versa.*

Gandhi wants to introduce the spinning-wheel in the education of the child because he finds no other dynamic and really effective means of drawing out the best out of the child. The spinning-wheel serves as the focal point of the child's growth and development of personality as it is elucidated in Figure 2.1.

The spinning-wheel, as Gandhi advocates in the education of the child, allows the child to comprehend all reactions derived from learning experiences in both theories and learning by doing. A certain sense of awareness is spontaneously developed in all possible directions as shown above. The learner, by his involvement in the spinning-wheel, negotiates general education and at the same time gives positive response to the

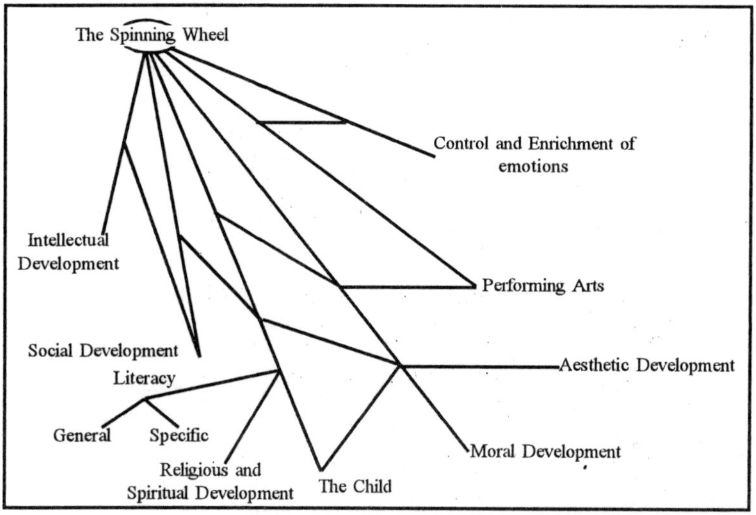

FIG. 2.1: Education of the child and the Spinning-wheel

diverse avenues of development—emotional, social, religious, spiritual, aesthetic and moral. Thus performing arts become intrinsic and invaluable in all-round development.

As for intellectual development of the child. Gandhi is conditional in affirming the fact that education always awaits a consolidating and practising means, and in that case, the spinning-wheel is both an invaluable means to an end-in-view of education and a thrilling vehicle for exercise of the incomparable power of appreciation. If the learner is allowed to exercise his power of imagination and appreciation in the manner best suited to himself in relation to others in and around him by means of the spinning-wheel, he will definitely discover an altogether new world of self-development and self-appreciation well geared to the excellence of personality.

Psychologically, the child is exposed to diverse emotional sensibilities like anger, fear, love, hate, anxiety, affection, cruelty etc. Gandhi launches the spinning-wheel in the education of the child to serve at least two psychological purposes. First, with involvement in the spinning-wheel, the child will be able to divert his emotional sensibilities towards manifestation of creativity and critical appreciation. Second, a certain form of adjustment to changing needs and a positive response to learning by doing are well administered by the spinning-wheel.

Gandhi also feels that education should cater to the child's aesthetic development. He, therefore, introduces the spinning-wheel which serves as an unending source of beauty and joy in the mind of the learner. The humming sound of the spinning-wheel provides the learner with the joy of creativity and wonder of self-manifestation. The fulness of education by means of the spinning-wheel as Gandhi envisages, becomes a pulsating reality.

Gandhi is also concerned with the education of the child from the sociological point of view. Hence, the importance of introducing the spinning-wheel in the education of the child. He makes spinning compulsory because it will enable the child to be in close touch with the living social reality. It will also contribute a great deal towards negotiating social imbalance and social superstition. Let the learner be allowed to devote to the spinning-wheel to be aware of social discrepancies and thereby practically learn how to play a little but significant role in ameliorating the distress of the downtrodden humanity.

Admittedly, Gandhi introduces the spinning-wheel in the sphere of education right at the early stage because he badly wants that every learner should be christened with the spirit of humanism from childhood. The softer sensibilities and finer visions of humanism in a child should, as he rightly asserts, be nursled from the earliest stage of education, and, in that case, the spinning-wheel definitely plays a very prominent and effective role. The thread that comes out of the spinning-wheel is the thread of global human unity born of genuine love and sincerity of purpose. The spinning-wheel is to education what blood is to the human body. This is neither a new fashion nor a new dogma, but a living reality even now in the context of dissociation of man and man in a so-called educated global society.

Gandhi's primary end-in-view of introducing the spinning-wheel in education is to make education relevant to life and living. Being distressed with appalling differences in rural life and urban life and being, in particular concerned with the dangerous apathy and ignorance shown towards rural handicrafts and rural vocations he introduces the spinning-wheel as a major breakthrough in the area of education for children in both rural and urban schools. This will, as he strongly believes, bring about a 'silent social revolution'. As a realistic reformer of social ukase and educational inconsistencies, he poignantly remarks:

> Today our villages have become a mere appendage to the cities. They exist, as it were, to be exploited by the latter and depend on the latter's sufferances. This is unnatural. It is only when the cities realize the duty of making an adequate return to the villages for

> the strength and sustenance which they derive from them, instead of selfishly exploiting them, that a healthy and moral relationship between the two will spring up. And if the city children are to play their part in the great and noble work of social reconstruction, the vocations through which they are to achieve their education ought to be directly related to the requirements of the villages. So far as I can see, the various processes of cotton manufacture from ginning and cleaning of cotton to the spinning of yarn, answer this test as nothing else does. Even today cotton is grown in the villages and is ginned and spun and converted into cloth in the cities. But the chain of processes which cotton undergoes in the mills from the beginning to the end constitutes a huge tragedy of waste in men, materials and mechanical power.
>
> My plan to impart primary education through the medium of village handicrafts like spinning and carding, etc. is thus conceived as the spearhead of a silent social revolution fraught with the most-far-reaching consequences. It will provide a healthy and moral basis of relationship between the city and the village and thus go a long way towards eradicating some of the worst evils of the present social insecurity and poisoned relationship between the classes.
>
> —M.K. Gandhi: *Harijan,* 9 October, 1937.

The education of true socialism as Gandhi wants to introduce by means of the spinning-wheel has its inner vision of maintenance of a certain sort of positive balance in the society. It is not only a symbol for the education of social harmony but also that of social awareness to build the solid foundation of global inter-relationship. As soon as the spinning-wheel will be a strong vehicle of aesthetic appreciation it will open out newer avenues for everyone to come closer to each other in respect of emotions, realities and sensibilities. Then, alone, the spinning-wheel will be a genuine progenitor of advancement of man and society.

The dynamic approach to education by means of introducing the spinning-wheel is neither a new one nor an outdated one even now as it has a viable proneness to be defeated in its very purpose due to misguided vision and paucity of sincere trained teachers.[1] But the plans and programmes of activities as Gandhi suggests in connection with the spinning-wheel in the course of Basic Education are significant:

> By means of this scheme *** we can make our boys self-confident and courageous. *Takli* will not be the only thing that will be taught

during the seven years. In the first year, we should teach the boys a little carding, even before the *takli.* Then the boys should be taught the collecting of cotton in the fields. After this, they can be taught spinning, first with *takli* and then with *charkha.* After spinning, the making of the *takli* and of the *charkha* should also be taught to the students.

— D.G. Tendulkar: *Mahatma,* Publications Division, Ministry of Information and Broadcasting, Government of India, 1969, Vol. IV, pp. 194-95.

To introduce the spinning wheel in the course of education as Gandhi does so in his scheme of Basic Education is to develop the child's inner vision of fulness and manifestation with all sincerity of purpose and action. Let the child be allowed through the spinning-wheel to develop the full man with him and behind this vision Gandhi wants to disseminate the lessons of self-confidence and self-esteem so important for development of personality and national regeneration of consciousness. Elucidating his Basic Education and the role of the spinning-wheel thereto, he observes:

My idea is not merely to teach a particular profession or occupation to the children, but to develop the full man through teaching that occupation. He will not only learn weaving, for instance, but learn why he should weave in a particular fashion and not any other, why he should handle yarn in a particular fashion and no other, and why he should himself know spinning and why should insist on a particular count for a particular kind of weaving. All these things the weaver boy does not learn at home. The spinning-wheel is to him just what it was a thousand years ago. We make him learn the art of making the most efficient wheel and a loom, not so as to displace another labour but so as to make them more efficient than the existing models. **** The working classes have all these centuries been isolated and relegated to the lower status. They have been *Shudras,* and the word has been interpreted to mean an inferior status. I want to allow no differentiation between the son of a weaver, of an agriculturist and of a school-master.

—*Ibid.,* p. 201.

A genuine iconoclast in the arena of education, Gandhi highlights the spinning-wheel not as a bare instrument to render variety or change in vocational education, but deep in his heart of hearts he realizes the most essential value of character and morality for which the spinning-wheel acts like a living mouthpiece. His primary objective to re-build the real 'man' in the learner so long eluded and despised can be well responded to by the spinning-wheel, provided that the latter is honoured and adored not as a teaching aid nor even as a teaching practice but certainly as a teaching principle well-followed by pupils with all earnestness and sincerity to consider it the wheel, as it were, of inward faith for the excellence of personality.

Gandhi advises pupils to stick to the spinning-wheel not only to learn as a course of education but also to undergo training in the habit of punctuality, cleanliness and systematized learning of excellence and quality. These will naturally lead to the fulness of man as the end-in-view of dynamic education. As he categorically remarks about the duties and responsibilities of the learners as spinners:

> They must all do sacrificial spinning in a scientific manner. Their tools will be always neat, clean, and in good order and condition. If possible, they will learn to make them themselves. Their yarn will naturally be of the highest quality. They will study the literature of spinning with all its economic, social, moral and political implications.
>
> — M.K. Gandhi: *Constructive Programmes,* Quoted in D.G. Tendulkar: *Mahatma,* Publications Division, Ministry of Information and Broadcasting, Government of India, 1969, Vol. VI, p. 30.

To allow pupils to probe deep into the study of the spinning-wheel, Gandhi himself has prepared sets of questions that will demand a clear concept in the knowledge of the technical aspects related to the spinning-wheel. In fact, the following questions as referred to by him in an article "what is Khadi Science?" are characteristic enough to prove his sincere endeavour at introducing the spinning-wheel from diverse dimensions:

1. Give a description of current Indian spinning-wheels. Which is the best among them? Give the drawing of any four spinning-wheels and the correct measurement of each constituent part. State of the species of wood employed, the length and girth of the spindle and the thickness of the *mal.*
2. Compare the current *Charkhas* with the Yeravda *Charkha* in the matter of speed, cost and general advantages.

3. How would you ascertain the variety of cotton, the strength of the yarn, and the count of spun yarn?
4. Of what count and strength is the yarn you spin? What is your speed on *takli* and wheel? Which wheel do you generally use?
5. How much cloth does a man and a woman require respectively for his or her clothing? How much yarn is required for making the same, and how much time is necessary for spinning it?
6. How much yarn is required to clothe the family? How much cotton is needed to produce the above? How much land is required for growing the necessary amount of cotton? (The family consists of a father and a mother and three children—one girl and two boys—seven, five and three years old.
7. Compare the current carding bow with the new ones. How much do you card per hour? How can you judge whether the cotton is properly carded or not? How many slivers do you make from one tola of cotton?
8. How much cotton can you gin in one hour? Compare ginning by hand with ginning by machine, giving the respective merits and demerits of either process. Describe and give a drawing of the current hand-ginning machine.
9. Give the length of the yarn of twenty counts required to weave one yard of cloth, 36 inches wide. How many hands are required to weave the same?
10. Compare the pit loom with the shuttle loom.

— D.G. Tendulkar: *Mahatma,* Publications Division, Ministry of Information and Broadcasting, Government of India, 1969, Vol. IV, pp. 120-21.

The spinning wheel is the focal point of education that preaches the universal truth: work is worship. Gandhi wants to introduce it in education to enable pupils to be genuine worshipper of mankind. Nevertheless, it is a strenuous but exciting endeavour at forging ahead with promises for fulness and emancipation of the best in everyone everywhere. Do we agree?

NOTE

1. Dr. Zakir Husain's observation in this respect is very relevant.

Mahatmaji thinks that the scheme which he has placed before you is absolutely original, and that it can be accepted only by those who believe in non-violence and in rural civilization. But those who are working in educational field will not find Mahatmaji's scheme very new. They know that true learning can be imparted only through doing. This method is called the Project Method in America and the Complex Method in Russia. We can certainly impart education to our children through the *takli* and the *charkha* and some other suitable handicrafts. But the greatest difficulty in carrying out this scheme will be the paucity of trained teachers. Professor Dewey in America had a similar plan which was welcomed enthusiastically, but he had to close down his school in three years, because he had no men to run it. Teachers may become slave-drivers and exploit the labour of poor boys. If this happens, *takli* would prove worse than the books and we shall be laying the foundation of hidden slavery in our country.

— D.G. Tendulkar: *Mahatma,* Publications Division, Ministry of Information and Broadcasting, Government of India, 1969, Vol. IV, p. 194.

3

SOCIETY AND THE SPINNING-WHEEL
Gandhian Inroads

A SOCIETY embraces communicated living of men with manifold traits of personality. This also encapsulates the idea that man is actually 'men' embodied in a single individual and *vice-versa.* As an unparalleled synchronizer and promoter of the ascent and excellence of man and society, Gandhi goes a step ahead to sing the victory of man, the *messiah* of the All Beautiful. He has a living faith in man who by means of the swan song of the spinning-wheel would be a permanent resident of the global society where whosoever he might be, he is honoured and endeared.

As a positive thinker of the emancipation of man in the society, Gandhi introduces the spinning-wheel essentially from three perspectives:

(a) The education of the spinning-wheel is one of restoration and dissemination of the true spirit of humanism in the society. Let the spirit of the nursling of the essential components of humanism be undertaken in right earnest by means of the spinning-wheel which binds man to man in the society. The spirit of unity so badly necessary for regeneration of mankind is most comprehensively and efficiently learnt and spread through it.

(b) The nurturing of the finer visions of man viz., fellow-feeling, kindness, pity, showing interest for others' welfare for the benefit of the person concerned with the spinning-wheel are also most easily and moderately possible.

(c) To re-enkindle the inner being is to re-vitalize the society. The spinning-wheel is the focal point of bringing about a silent social revolution to ensure this re-enkindling of the inner being of everyone in the society.

The 'life-giving sun' as Gandhi characteristically identifies it, the spinning-wheel alone can bring back and restore faith of a marooned society. This is why he advocates it as the guiding force and boosting agent or mouth-piece of other handicrafts in the society. On February, 10, 1938, while opening the All-India Village Industries and Khadi Exhibition, he emphasizes on the significant role of the spinning-wheel in the society, which can definitely ensure one's decent approach to earn bread, and this has been further elucidated by him at Haripura where he categorically states:

> I have often said that if seven lakhs of the villages of India were to be kept alive, and if peace that is at the root of civilization is to be achieved, we have to make the spinning-wheel the centre of all handicrafts. Thus my faith in the spinning-wheel is growing every day and I see it more and more clearly that the sun of the spinning-wheel will alone illumine the planets of other handicrafts. But I go further and say that just as we go on discovering the new stars and planets in the vast solar system, even so we should go on discovering fresh handicrafts everyday. But for the sake of this thing we shall have to make the spinning-wheel the really life-giving sun.
>
> —D.G. Tendulkar: *Mahatma,* Publications Division, Ministry of Information and Broadcasting, Government of India, 1969, Vol. IV, pp. 215-16.

From a historical and social perspective, the spinning-wheel serves a very important role among the masses even now. Gandhi reminds us of the fact that whatever consciousness it brings forth in socio-economic patterns of life is always a positive factor in humanistic development. It even now makes us aware of the fact that true nationalism is born amidst the humming sound of the spinning-wheel in every corner of rural India where the seeds of national and social cohesion are to be sown through the music of the spinning-wheel. The role of *Khadi* as Gandhi allows to thrive in war footing is in essence a symbolic mouthpiece of the spinning-wheel in making a constructive and purposeful foundation of an emerging socio-political and socio-economic regeneration of mankind.[1] It also characterizes the fact that a silent social revolution is best spearheaded by the spinning-wheel.

A foreseer of social change, Gandhi emphasizes on hand-spinning not with a view to aiming at any replacement of or competing with any machinery but to evoke the inherent power of self-confidence and self-esteem in every member of the society. It is a completely practicable and easily adaptable form of bringing about a definite pattern of change in life and society. In fact, the spinning-wheel as a purposeful remunerative occupation changes the mind-set of every one more or less suffering from a certain kind of inferiority complex in the society. Moreover, the spinning-wheel binds the heart of everyone in the society with the common cord of social oneness. To eliminate idleness and laziness of rural people in particular due to absence of work it has, as Gandhi rightly asserts, practically no alternative so immediate, arresting, lively and appealing. In his own words,

> Hand-spinning does not, it is not intended that it should, compete with, in order to displace, any existing type of industry, it does not aim at withdrawing a single able-bodied person, who can otherwise find a remunerative occupation from his work. The sole claim advanced on its behalf is that it alone offers an immediate, practicable, and permanent solution of that problem of problems, that confronts India, viz., the enforced idleness for nearly six months in the year of an overwhelming majority of India's population, owing to lack of a suitable supplementary occupation to agriculture and the chronic starvation of the masses that results therefrom.
>
> — M.K. Gandhi: *Young India,* 21 October, 1926.

What Gandhi expressed some seven decades ago as a rough estimate has more or less a relevance in the changed socio-economic perspective at present in so far as the spinning-wheel is promising and prospective in nurturing cottage industry with a fine blending of talent and practice in art and culture, tradition and individuality, Gandhi's own explanation in this connection is :

> I would favour the use of the most elaborate machinery if thereby India's pauperism and resulting idleness be avoided. I have suggested hand-spinning as the only ready means of driving away penury and making famine of work and wealth impossible. The spinning-wheel itself is a piece of valuable machinery, and in my own humble way I have tried to secure improvement in it in keeping with the special conditions of India.
>
> —M.K. Gandhi: *Young India,* 3 November, 1921.

Elsewhere, Gandhi is more explicit in forewarning us against rampant use of machinery at the invaluable loss of human ingenuity and potentiality so essential for maintenance and enrichment of social cohesion and social balance:

> Machinery has its place, it has come to stay. But it must not be allowed to displace necessary human labour. An improved plough is a good thing. But if by some chances, one man could plough up by some mechanical invention of his the whole of the land of India, and control all the agricultural produce and if the millions had no other occupation, they would starve, and being idle, they would become dunces, as many have already become. There is hourly danger of many more being reduced to that unenviable state.
>
> I would welcome every improvement in the cottage machine, but I know that it is criminal to displace hand-labour by the introduction of power-driven spindles unless one is at the same time ready to give millions of farmers some other occupation in their homes.
>
> —M.K. Gandhi, *Young India,* 5 November, 1925.

Again, Gandhi has also the practical end-in-view of raising the status of women in our country who for no fault of their own are more or less deprived of education and esteem in the social atmosphere in every nook and corner. That they should be allowed to enjoy a dignified position in the society can be well advanced in associating them with the spinning-wheel. Hence, the importance of *Khadi* for social and national awareness and prosperity. In this connection, it is interesting to note Gandhi's own observation:

> There is no doubt that *Khadi* cannot compete with mill cloth, it was never meant to. If the people will not understand or appreciate the law governing *Khadi,* it will never be universal. It must then remain the fad of the monied people and cranks. And if it is to be merely that, the labours of a huge organization like the All-India Spinners' Association must mean a waste of effort, if not something much worse.
>
> But *Khadi* has a big mission. *Khadi* provides dignified labour to the millions who are otherwise idle for nearly four months in the year. Even apart from the remuneration the work brings, it is its own reward. For if millions live in compulsory idleness, they must die spiritually, mentally and physically. The spinning-wheel automatically raises the status of the millions of poor women.

Even though, therefore, the mill cloth were to be given gratis to the people, their true welfare demands that they should refuse to have it in preference to *Khadi,* the product of their labour.

Life is more than money. It is cheaper to kill our aged parents who can do no work and who are a drag on our slender resources. It is also cheaper to kill our children whom we do not need for our material comfort and whom we have to maintain without getting anything in return. But we neither kill our parents nor our children, but consider it a privilege to maintain them no matter what their maintenance costs us. Even so must we maintain *Khadi* to the exclusion of all other cloth. It is the force of habit which makes us think of *Khadi* in terms of prices. We must revise our notion of *Khadi* economics. When we have studied them from the point of view of national well-being, we shall find that *Khadi* is never dear.

—D.G. Tendulkar: *Mahatma,* Publications Division, Ministry of Information and Broadcasting, Government of India, 1969, Vol. IV, pp. 307-308.

The socialization of man by means of introducing the spinning-wheel vigorously as Gandhi actually does so has a far reaching effect in boosting the morale of the masses. Naturally, the spirit of patriotism so essential for men and women in the society finds a new language of expression by means of the introduction of the spinning-wheel. This is a historical fact that Gandhi launches right from 1918 in India for reawakening of the spirit of patriotism—dynamic and practical—in the society. Moral and social elevation with a 'living faith' in God by taking recourse to the spinning-wheel as he suggests at the Faizpur Congress on 27 December 1936 is the only alternative to forged values and duped society. In his own words,

It is not enough that one wears *Khadi* on the ceremonial occasions or even wears it to the exclusion of all other cloth, if he surrounds himself with *Videshi* in everything else. *Khadi* means the truest *Swadeshi* spirit, identification with the starving millions.

Let there be no mistake about my conception of *Swaraj.* It is complete independence of alien control and complete economic independence. So, at one end you have political independence, at the other the economic. It has two other ends. One of them is moral and social, the corresponding end is *dharma,* that is, religion in the highest sense of the term. It includes Hinduism, Islam, Christianity etc. but is superior to them all. You may recognize it

> by the name of Truth, not the honesty of expedience but the living Truth that pervades everything and will survive all destruction and all transformation. The moral and social uplift may be recognized by the term we are used to, that is, non-violence. Let us call this the square of *Swaraj,* which will be out of shape if any of its angles is untrue.
>
> —*Ibid.,* p. 114.

To identify oneself with everyone in the society through the spinning-wheel as Gandhi advocates is one of the fundamental lessons of humanistic socialism which has its importance even now under a changing concept of globalised socialism. Gandhi wants to be assured of a well-balanced society where every-one is well-employed. And if this is so, he is ready to eliminate the role of the spinning-wheel in relation to man and society. As he categorically observes,

> I have not contemplated, much less advised, the abandonment of a single healthy, life-giving industrial activity for the sake of hand-spinning. The entire foundation of the spinning-wheel rests on the fact that there are crores of semi-employed people in India. And I should admit that if there were none such, there would be no room for the spinning-wheel.
>
> —M.K. Gandhi: *Young India,* 27 May, 1926.

Elsewhere, Gandhi clarifies doubts and misgivings about the spinning-wheel as a vital instrument of social change as follows:

> The spinning-wheel is undoubtedly mediaeval, but it seems to have come to stay. Though this article is the same, it has become a symbol of freedom and unity as at one time, after the advent of the East India Company, it had become the symbol of slavery. Modern India has found in it a deeper and truer meaning than our forefathers had dreamt of. Even so, if the handicrafts were once symbols of factory labour, may they now be symbols and vehicles of education in the fullest and truest sense of the term.
>
> —M.K. Gandhi, *Harijan,* 16 October, 1937.

Admittedly, Gandhi gives a new dimension of *Khadi* and the spinning-wheel by highlighting the true spirit of *Khadi* as a science for understanding and appreciating man and society. In fact, the three great ills of the society—pauperism, idleness and unemployment—as he particularly identifies can be significantly handled with the spinning-wheel and *Khadi.* In his own elucidation in an article. "What is *Khadi* Science", he observes:

> I have often said that if *Khadi* is a sound economic proposition it is also a science and a romance. I believe there is a book *The Romance of Cotton* wherein the origin of cotton has been traced and an attempt made to show how its discovery altered the course of civilization. Everything can be turned into a science or a romance, if there is a scientific or a romantic spirit behind it. Some people scoff at *Khadi* and betray signs of impatience or disgust, when one talks of spinning. But it ceases to be an object of disgust of ridicule, immediately you attribute to it the power of removing India-wide idleness, unemployment and consequent pauperism. It need not be, as a matter of fact, a panacea for the three ills. To be absorbingly interesting, the mere honest attributing of the power is enough. But you cannot attribute that potency of *Khadi* and pursue it, as some do, in the manner of an ignorant needy artisan, who gins, cards, spins or weaves, because he must for his bread. A believer in its potency will pursue it in a deliberate, wise, methodical manner and in a scientific spirit, taking nothing for granted, testing every proposition, checking facts and figures, undaunted by defeats, unelated by petty successes, never satisfied till the goal is reached.
>
> —D.G. Tendulkar: *Mahatma,* Publications Division, Ministry of Information and Broadcasting, Government of India, 1969, Vol. IV, p. 119.

As an introspective social visionary who practically goes deep into the socio-economic condition of the masses. Gandhi draws our attention to down-to-earth matters of life. He advocates for the introduction of the spinning-wheel among these hapless people to christen them in the spirit of self-help and self-reliance which allow them to earn and restore dignity in living in the society. In fact, the spinning-wheel becomes the wheel of social regeneration of living in a worthwhile manner. Gandhi adroitly draws our attention to this fact of self-reliance by means of the spinning-wheel in the following inimitable words:

> A starving man thinks first of satisfying his hunger before anything else. He will sell his liberty and all for the sake of getting a morsel of food. Such is the position of millions of the people of India. For them, liberty, God and all such words are merely letters put together

> without the slightest meaning. They jar upon them. If we want to give these people a sense of freedom we shall have to provide them with work which they can easily do it their desolate homes and which would give them at least the barest living. This can only be done by the spinning-wheel. And when they have become self-reliant and are able to support themselves, we are in a position to talk to them about freedom, about Congress, etc.
>
> —M.K. Gandhi, *Young India,* 18 March, 1926.

It is interesting to note in this connection that as a true social visionary. Gandhi foresees Indian independence in the light of social self-reliance, where everyone is concerned with the welfare of others and the spinning-wheel serves a major role in this direction. Moreover, it baptises one to be conscious of oneself not only in the spirit of self-identity but also in the most desirable spirit of oneness and nationality which is endangered in the midst of unwanted affluence.

With a scientific, liberal and broad-minded awareness to life and society, Gandhi, as more often misunderstood than not, is never against reality nor does he ever nursle the spirit of utopia in making the society blessed with all self-sufficient people. In fact, he never thinks of the liberation of India with the power of the spinning-wheel which does not embrace the diverse sciences associated with it. Tracing back to the history of introducing the spinning-wheel, he emphasises on the importance of a scientific bent of mind whereby newer avenues of understanding and appreciating the role of the spinning-wheel in a changing society is better identified:

> When I first discovered the spinning-wheel, it was purely through intuition. It was not backed by knowledge, so much so that I confused the *Charkha* with handloom. Later on, however, I tried to work out its possibilities with the help of the late Maganlal Gandhi. For instance, the question arose. Why should the spindle be made of iron, and not of brass? Should it be thin or thick? What would be the proper thickness? We began with the mill spindles. Then, spindle-holders used to be bamboo and wood. Later we came to leather and gut bearings. It was found that the spindles got easily bent and were difficult to straighten. So we tried to make them out of the knitting needles and ultimately of the umbrella wires. All this called for the exercise of the inventive faculty and scientific research.
>
> A *Khadi* worker with a scientific mind will not stop there.

> 'Why the spinning-wheel, why not the spinning-mill?' he will ask himself. The reply will be that everybody cannot own a spinning mill. If people depend on the spinning-mills for their clothing, whoever controls the spinning-mills will control them, and thus there will be an end to the individual liberty. Today, anyone can reduce the whole of London and New York to submission within twenty-four hours by cutting off their electric and water supply. Individual liberty and inter-dependence are both essential for life in society. Only a Robinson Crusoe can afford to be all self-sufficient. When a man has done all he can for the satisfaction of his essential requirements, then he will seek the co-operation of his neighbours for the rest. That will be the true co-operation. Thus a scientific study of the spinning-wheel will lead on to sociology. The spinning-wheel will not become a power for the liberation of India in our hands, unless we have made a deep study of the various sciences related to it. It will not only then make India free, but point the way to the whole world.
>
> —D.G. Tendulkar, *Mahatma,* Publications Division, Ministry of Information and Broadcasting, Government of India, 1969, Vol. VII, p. 37.

As a vehicle of social emergence, the spinning-wheel as Gandhi feels, makes inroads to awareness so necessary for dealing with the realities of life. What he wants as a forewarning against passivities and drabness is to be always on the alert to utilize every moment of life, and, in this particular end-in-view, the spinning-wheel becomes the wheel of dynamism in social upbringing of man. The bond of a common will to accept the direct challenge of life against poverty and indolence, with which the individual is christened by the spinning-wheel goes a long way in rebuilding the mansion of humane sensibilities in social advancement.

Gandhi points out a negotiable relationship between *Khadi* and the spinning-wheel without which the former has no importance in life and society. Mere concentration on *Khadi* as it is found in present day even would lead to 'a decent burial' as he forecasts in a very significant way. The introduction of the spinning-wheel in the society would alone give life-blood to handloom in industry and people engaged in it would find an appropriate avenue of social advancement. As Gandhi warns,

> In hand-spun yarn lies its (the handloom industry) only salvation. If the spinning-wheel goes, the handloom is bound to follow suit.

> *Khadi* will cease to have any value in my eyes if it does not usefully employ the millions. Many of the 'compromises' that have been suggested are such as to take away from it its essential character. The late Sir Fazalbhai prophesied to me, when I saw him thirty years ago, that *Khadi* was ultimately bound to fail. He is gone, but *Khadi* has remained. May be a new era has now opened and *Khadi* is an anachronism in it. Only, I do not feel so.
>
> —D.G. Tendular: *Mahatma,* Publications Division, Ministry of Information and Broadcasting, Government of India, 1969, Vol. VII, p. 187.

To forewarn man and society as Gandhi does by introducing the spinning-wheel, against the aggravating spirit of industrialization and rampant use of machinery, is actually to forewarn against the rise of capitalism and the anarchy of affluence which is indeed the curse of society.

Therefore, the spinning-wheel of Gandhi actually endeavours at stands for a protest against 'machinery as a whole.'[2] He also pleads for considering the spinning-wheel a 'spinning-mill in miniature' so that the appalling economic deprivation and unemployment writ large in society be well arrested. In this connection his own words on the occasion of the opening ceremony of the Magan Museum of *Khadi* and other village crafts and the Udyog Bhawan at Wardha on December 30, 1938 are very significant:

> I admit that in terms of orthodox and stereotyped standards of economics, as that science is understood and taught in our colleges today, and in a society governed by those standards, village industries including spinning, have, perhaps, no chance, and to revive them might appear like reversion to the Middle Ages. But I would like you to enter the Udyog Bhawan with a fresh and unsophisticated mind that has shed all its prejudices. Envisage this spinning-wheel as a spinning-mill in miniature that enables a person to earn two annas daily in his home in this land of chronic and nation-wide unemployment and starvation, when otherwise he would not be earning two pice even. Picture this mill planted in lakhs of homes, as it is capable of being planted, and I see nothing in the world which can compete with it.
>
> —D.G. Tendulkar: *Mahatma,* Publications Division, Ministry of Information and Broadcasting, Government of India, 1969, Vol. V, p. 7.

Like a liberal and ardent connoisseur of social change. Gandhi never wants to introduce the spinning-wheel rigidly nor does he want to involve men and women in the society to undertake the responsibility of bringing about a social change in a half-hearted manner. In fact, he advises to take up the spinning-wheel as an effective tool for social regeneration. Therefore, he alone can categorically assert:

> Wind up the All-India Spinners' Association as a centralised organisation for the production and distribution of *Khadi.* Let it function solely as the custodian of the values for which *Khadi* stands and as a central research organisation for providing technical assistance and moral guidance to the local organisations.
>
> * * * * *
>
> Some say that the new rule will in fact kill the *Khadi* which the poor are now producing and that only a few fashionable town dwellers will spin and have cloth woven for themselves. *** The masses do not eat for show but only in order that they may live. They wear clothes to cover their nakedness, not to be fashionable. Therefore, the spinning-wheel, like the oven, should find a place in every village home and every able-bodied person should spin.
>
> —Pyarelal: *Mahatma Gandhi: The Last Phase,* Navajivan Publishing House, Ahmedabad, 1965, Vol. I, Book I, p. 53.

Time and again Gandhi refers to the fact that *Khadi* and for that end-in-view the spinning-wheel are the positive means of revival of strength among the masses in every nook and corner of the society. Emancipation of man and society from exploitation, indeed, awaits the right role of the spinning-wheel. This is why he emphasizes on the fact that true *Swaraj* is almost entirely dependent on the true role of the spinning-wheel in the entire society. In his own words,

> Everyone should realize that it is wrong to consider *Khadi* as merely a means of livelihood. If it were only an industry it ought to be run on commercial lines. The mills provide a livelihood to thousands, if not lakhs, in one city. Through *Khadi* we put crores of rupees into the pockets of 15,000 villages. That is the only difference between the two. Regarded in this light, the case for the use of *Khadi* to the exclusion of mill cloth loses much of its force. And the claim of *Khadi* as a means of attaining *Swaraj* also falls to the ground. But the ideal of *Khadi* has always been as a means,

> *par excellence,* for the resuscitation of villages and there through the generation of real strength among the masses–the strength that will *ipso facto* bring *Swaraj.*
>
> — M.K. Gandhi: *Swaraj Through Charkha,* compiled by Kanu Gandhi, All India Spinners' Association, Sevagram, 1945, p. 8.

The vision of the spinning-wheel as Gandhi wants to disseminate is the vision of an enlightened society free from narrowness and biased approach to life. Man here is the ideal exponent and saviour of 'men', and *vice versa.* Man here is transformed and transcended towards fulness of growth, fulness of unity and fulness of personality. The home within every man is the vast abode of social peace and sanctity, perfection and purity. The spinning-wheel, therefore, is the life-blood in which the hopes and aspirations are distilled in detachment. Gandhi is always against bartering of whatever is prejudicial to society. Rather would he probe deep into all the problems afflicting the society. In fact, the spinning-wheel is meant not merely for spinning as such but also the serene devotion to spinning for the goodness of the entire society irrespective of caste, creed, community etc. Let the humming sound of the spinning-wheel fulfil the vision he so cherishes in the words of the song.

We are inhabitants of a country
  where there is no sorrow or suffering,
Where there is no illusion nor anguish,
  no delusion nor desire,
Where flows the Ganges of love
  and the whole creation is full of joy,
Where all minds flow in one direction,
  and where there is no occasion for sense of time,
All have their wants satisfied;
Here all barrier is just,
Here all are cast in the same mould,
Here is no lack nor care,
No selfishness in any shape or form,
No high no low, no master no slave;
All is right, yet no burning heat,
That country is within you—
  It is *Swaraj, Swadeshi,*
The home is within you—

Victory! Victory! Victory!
He realises it who longs for it.

—Pyarelal: *Mahatma Gandhi: The Last Phase,* Navajivan Publishing House, Ahmedabad, 1965, Vol. I, Book I, p. 182.

NOTES

1. An interpretation of *Khadi* and, for that end-in-view, of the spinning-wheel from this standpoint by Zealey is very significant.

   Of all the non-violent weapons forged by Gandhi, *Khadi* was the nearest moral equivalent of the infantryman's rifle. It was conducive to national solidarity. It provided the lowliest with a weapon of defence, which on a mass scale was formidable. Also like the infantryman's rifle it was a powerful and meaningful symbol.

   At the time of its inception, the constructive programme on *Khadi* was indeed a stroke of genius, making an important contribution to several important needs within the independence movement. *Nationally,* it provided a rallying symbol which the humblest villager could easily understand. *Politically* it was a powerful weapon providing a means whereby a sense of united action could be expressed in concrete form. *Economically* it was a means whereby the formidable problem of rural under-development would be turned to productive use.

   — Philip Zealey: "Comments on Khadi", *Gandhi Marg,* Journal of the Gandhi Peace Foundation, New Delhi, Vol. 2, No. 4, p. 295.

2. Julius Braunthal, the celebrated Austrian socialist, makes a very significant observation in this respect:

   Gandhi's efforts are directed not only against the industrial manufacture of textiles, but ultimately against all industry, against machinery as a whole; but here, too, his views are more in accordance with the specific positions of India than might appear at first.

   Gandhi ..... rejects machinery only because, instead of saving the work of the individual and alleviating conditions of life for the community, it is now useful only to a minority of rich men, and inflicts infinite harm on the working masses. And as in Gandhi's eyes benefit or injury to the masses, to the poor and needy, is the sole criterion for judging every institution this recognition of the fatal effect of industrialism on the masses leads him to reject machinery.

   The occidental may call it the attempt of a *petit bourgeois* reactionary, and it even appears as such if objectively regarded from a more advanced historical stage; but if it is looked at from the angle of the peculiar historical development and the social and economic conditions of India, this rebellion against capitalism assumes greater revolutionary significance than, say, the rebellion of the Luddites against machinery.

   The hatred of machinery, the hatred of capitalism, which burns so strongly in Gandhi, is the reflection of the hate of millions of Indian peasants and handworkers, whose traditional basis of existence was completely destroyed by capitalism and who were excluded from the possibility of existence on a capitalist basis as a factory proletariat.

   — Julius Braunthal: *Mahatma Gandhi and Indian Revolution,* Quoted in Rene Fulop-Miller, *Lenin and Gandhi,* F.S. Flint and D.F. Tait (Translated), Putnam, London, pp. 228-234.

4

NON-VIOLENCE AND THE SPINNING-WHEEL
Gandhian Points of Unison

THE SPINNING-WHEEL as Mahatma Gandhi incorporates in his philosophy of man is the symbol of emancipation. It is that emancipation which indicates how man should strive for fulness. When Gandhi associates non-violence with the spinning-wheel, he actually makes a unison of worship with work. Work as work is meaningless. But when it responds to the soul of consciousness as he actually wants to arrive at by means of the fundamental ends-in-view of the spinning-wheel, it adores Truth, Beauty and Goodness.

Admittedly, Gandhi's main concern with non-violence as a positive force of social welfare is never a trickery nor a sentimental patch-work for peace and harmony but an involvement to be always in tune with practice and discipline. Therefore, any failure in the exercise of the spirit of non-violence definitely refers to the inherent inconsistencies with which every human being is more or less constrained. Gandhi wants to introduce the spinning-wheel to revive that spirit where non-violence becomes a strong positive force well nourished in self-help and self-support.

The Civil Disobedience Movement—the *Satyagraha*—as Gandhi wants to highlight should embrace the spinning-wheel in all non-violent principles of action. Otherwise, *Swaraj* as he categorically asserts, will be a mere sentimental endeavour to social and national awakening. A desirable and worthwhile pattern of coherence in all affairs of life awaits cohesion between one state and the other within the country. This is undeniably a compulsory pre-condition to launch any movement in a non-violent manner, and this pre-condition is very well negotiated by means of infusing the inherent spirit of the spinning-wheel. In this connection, Gandhi's viewpoints on the desirable role of the *Satyagrahis* in his article "Jaipur Civil Disobedience" in March, 1939 are significant:

> *Swaraj* within the Indian states is not to be obtained by any non-violent trick. It will be won, if it is to be won, by non-violence of the strong, that is, by hard work, by patient and mute suffering, by service of the poor, the hungry and the forsaken of society, and a voluntary obedience to the laws of the state and society, in so far as they are not repugnant to public and private morals. Unless non-violence of the strong is really developed among us, there should be no thought of civil disobedience for *Swaraj,* whether within the states or in British India. As indispensable test—by no means infallible—of non-violence, I adhere to habitual spinning and habitual use of *Khadi* by the would-be civil resister. The Jaipur *Satyagrahis,* if they desire to take part in any civil disobedience struggle that may take place in future, should understand the implications of non-violence and apply themselves with zest to the fulfilment of the minimum conditions I have prescribed. Let them also know that what applies to them applies to all *Satyagrahis* that I may have to deal with.
>
> —D.G. Tendulkar: *Mahatma,* Publications Division, Ministry of Information and Broadcasting, Government of India, 1969, Vol. V, pp. 70-71.

The principle of non-violence should, as Gandhi asserts, be principle of 'selfless service of the masses' and to adhere to this principle sincerely is to correlate non-violence with the spinning-wheel. It should be remembered that Gandhi considers the spinning-wheel the best symbol of non-violence. In his own words,

> *Ahimsa* must express itself through the acts of selfless service of the masses. I cannot think of a better symbol of, or medium, for its expression than the spinning-wheel.
>
> —D.G. Tendulkar: *Mahatma,* Publications Division, Ministry of Information and Broadcasting, Government of India, 1969, Vol. V, p. 81.

While advocating the progress of the spinning-wheel and, for that end-in-view, of *Khadi,* Gandhi highlights the spirit of non-violence in terms of reality. He is aware of the fact that there is always an aversion to the spinning-wheel and the *Khadi* by town-dwellers and people living in cities but he insists on facing the reality as it would unmask all ignorance and, in his own words,

> *** It will still be a triumph for truth, because it will be clear that the people had no real faith in non-violence and that they wore *Khadi* out of ignorance and deceived themselves into thinking that thereby they would obtain *Swaraj.* The special claim for *Khadi* is that it is an unrivalled means for rescuing the masses from the idleness and inertia in which they are today plunged and for creating the necessary strength in them for winning through.
>
> — M.K. Gandhi: *Swaraj Through Charkha,* compiled by Kanu Gandhi, All India Spinners Association, Sevagram, Wardha, 1945.

Moreover, Gandhi also advises to cast off all fear related to *Khadi* and the spinning-wheel, and encourages to be inspired with the true spirit of self-rule in a non-violent but valiant way. The challenge of the spinning-wheel to overcome all constraints related to popularizing *Khadi* in a non-violent manner is a challenge to be undertaken with a single-minded devotion to stick-to-itiveness. It stands for a living faith born and nurtured with the spirit of non-violence. As Gandhi advises.

> Unless you can cast out this fear from your hearts it will spell the death of *Khadi* for *Swaraj. Khadi* has established for itself a prestige in society. The rich feel a pride in purchasing *Khadi* produced by the poor. But that is very little. If you restrict the scope of *Khadi* to no more than a source of relief to the poor, it will not help you to obtain *Swaraj* through non-violence. I do not want such a thing to happen but I would not mind if as a result of enforcing the rule about the sale of *Khadi* against yarn I am left the sole wearer of *Khadi.* *** It would be better for *Khadi* to die a natural death, if that is God's will, than that it should be killed by our cowardice and lack of faith.
>
> — *Ibid.*

To be christened with the spirit of the spinning-wheel is, according to Gandhi to be in the track of non-violence, and unless a *Satyagrahi* is tuned with its living spirit, his very objective of *Satyagraha* is utterly defeated. A living faith in the spinning-wheel always stands for a symbol of non-violence. Gandhi's words of address to the members of the Gandhi Seva Sangh at Brindaban in 1939 reveal this poignant truth.

> How many of you have a living faith in the spinning-wheel? Do you believe in it as a symbol of non-violence? If we had that faith, our spinning would have a potency all its own. Spinning is even more potent than Civil Disobedience. The latter may provoke anger and ill-will. Spinning-provokes no such feeling. My faith in the spinning-wheel I declared twenty years ago. I am declaring it again with the added strength of my twenty years' experience. If you feel that you have no such faith I would again ask you to forget *Satyagraha.*
>
> *   *   *   *   *
>
> I am not talking of the thousands of our starving sisters who must spin for their daily bread, but I am talking of those who profess to believe in truth and non-violence. The moment they realize that spinning is the symbol of non-violence, it will serve as a beacon light to them, it will inspire all their conduct, they will regard all waste of time as criminal, their language will be free of all offensive expression and they will not think an idle thought.
>
> — D.G. Tendulkar: *Mahatma*, Publications Division, Ministry of Information and Broadcasting, Government of India, 1969, Vol. V, p. 92.

A year later, Gandhi reiterates the spinning-wheel as a symbol of non-violence and expresses his firm conviction on it and also explains how it can be 'a true sacrificial act'.

> I may be wrong, in the eyes of others, in my belief that with every thread that I draw I am bringing *Swaraj* nearer, but for me the belief is as true as the fact that I exist. That saves me from losing my sanity. This spinning-wheel is a symbol of non-violence for me. The wheel as such is lifeless, but when I invest it with symbolism, it becomes a living thing for me. Its sound, if it is musical, is in tune with non-violence. If it is unmusical, it is not in tune with it, for it indicates carelessness on my part. The steel spindle one can use as a deadly weapon, but we have put it there for the best possible use. So we have to be meticulously careful about every part of the wheel. Then and then only, will it produce fine music and spinning-wheel will be a true sacrificial act.
>
> —*Ibid.*, p. 290

The relationship between *Khadi* and *Swaraj* or between non-violence and the spinning-wheel as Gandhi time and again asserts, is very close. Such a close relationship makes a living faith in Truth all the more comprehensive and relevant to life. Bearing in mind the appalling distress of millions of rural people, Gandhi encourages the spread of the spinning-wheel as an appropriate tool for negotiating all challenges in a non-violent manner. This non-violent means may not be looked upon well by the affluent town-dwellers. But the challenges of untoward situations like non-co-operation in any form whatsoever should be boldly faced and negotiated by sticking to Truth or non-violence even at the cost of life. Gandhi categorically unfold this inseparable relationship between the spinning-wheel and non-violence as follows:

> An increase in the number of mills and cities will certainly not contribute to the prosperity of India's millions. On the contrary, it will bring further poverty to the unemployed and all the diseases that follow in the wake of starvation. If town-dwellers can look upon such a spectacle with equanimity there is nothing more to be said. In such an event it will be the reign of violence in India, not a reign of Truth and *Ahimsa*. And we shall be forced to admit that there is naturally no room there for *Khadi*. Military training will then have to be compulsory for all. But we must only think in terms of the starving crores. If they are to be restored, if they are to live, then the *Charkha* must be made the central activity and people must spin voluntarily. The weapon of non-violence may not, however, be taken up because there is no alternative to it. There must be faith in it. The rule of yarn for the purchase of *Khadi* must not only come into force but must increase in its application.
>
> — M.K. Gandhi: *Swaraj Through Charkha,* compiled by Kanu Gandhi, All India Spinners' Association, Sevagram, Wardha, 1945, p. 5

To replace non-violence by coercion or violence in order to popularize the spinning-wheel among the masses is alien to the life and philosophy of Mahatma Gandhi. In fact, he strongly advocates non-violence in the dissemination of the spinning-wheel and, as such, admits that the death of non-violence in the form of its failure to guide the spinning-wheel as the most potent symbol is actually his own death as a baffled exponent of humanism. Continuing his argument in favour of synthesizing non-violence with the spinning-wheel a little more, he categorically states:

> If, on account of it, the existing *bhandars* have to close down and *Khadi*-wearers give up *Khadi,* it will still be a triumph of Truth because it will be clear that people had no real faith in non-violence and that they wore *Khadi* out of ignorance and deceived themselves into thinking that thereby they would obtain *Swaraj.* When I know that such *Khadi* will never obtain *Swaraj* and even if *Swaraj* is attained it will immediately be discarded, how can I allow people to continue to deceive themselves? In that case the prophecy of the late Shri Chintamani will come true that on Gandhiji's death people will dislike him and his spinning-wheel to such an extent that they will throw out *Charkhas* from their homes to make his funeral pyre. If hand-spun yarn is not in fact a symbol of non-violence then I should retrieve my error during my life-time and save, at any rate, the wood of the *Charkhas.*
>
> —*Ibid.*

Of the four-fold constructive programme which Gandhi advocates for cultivation of non-violence in thought, word and deed, the spinning-wheel is the central point of interest. Why does he give maximum importance to the spinning-wheel in the practice of non-violence? The answer is clear and simple. It alone harmoniously blends life with work and *vice-versa.* In his advice to the workers he remarks:

> Maximum of work and minimum of speech must be your motto. In the centre of the programme is the spinning-wheel–no haphazard programme of spinning but scientific understanding of every detail, including the mechanics and the mathematics of it, study of cotton and its varieties, and so on.
>
> —D.G. Tendulkar: *Mahatma*, Publications Division, Ministry of Information and Broadcasting, Government of India, 1969, Vol. V, p. 112.

The power of the spinning-wheel which Gandhi alone visualizes and wants to make the entire mankind to visualize is the functional and the most effective power to restore and boost communal and national harmony. In fact, without a vigorous exercise of the spirit inherent in the spinning-wheel, his very idea of non-violence as an incomparable integrating force remains either misunderstood or an illusion. Addressing the executive members of the Gandhi Seva Sangh on 25 October 1939, he unfolds the spirit of non-violence in terms of that of the spinning-wheel, and advises to have a firm faith on the latter to combat against disunity, economic exploitation and other disruptive forces affecting *Swaraj* and rural people.

> Non-violence is not a cloistered virtue, confined only to the *rishi* and the care-dweller. It is capable of being practised by the millions, not with full knowledge of all its implications, but because it is the law of our species. It distinguishes man from the brute. But, man has not shed the brute in him. He has to strive to do so. This striving applies to the practice of non-violence, not to the belief in it. I cannot strive to believe in a principle; I either believe in it or I do not. And if I believe in it, I must bravely strive to practise it. *Ahimsa* is an attribute of the brave. Cowardice and *Ahimsa* don't go together any more than water and fire. And it is that *Ahimsa* that every member of the Gandhi Seva Sangh has to make conscious effort to develop in himself.
>
> We have often thought about this question, but the hour of our trial has arrived today, as much with reference to the Hindu-Muslim unity. And remember also that your non-violence cannot operate effectively, unless you have faith in the spinning-wheel. I would ask you to read *Hind Swaraj* with my eyes and see therein the chapter on how to make India non-violent. You cannot build non-violence on a factory civilization, but you can build it on self-contained villages. Even if Herr Hitler was so minded, he could not devastate 700,000 non-violent villages. He would himself become non-violent in the process. Rural economy, as I have conceived it, eschews exploitation altogether, and exploitation is the essence of violence. You have, therefore, to be rural minded, before you can be non-violent, and to be rural-minded you have to have full faith in the spinning-wheel.
>
> —*Ibid.*, pp. 189-190.

If non-violence is, as Gandhi time and again interprets, the Divine Law of Love, the spinning-wheel represents that love in the best possible manner. The latter not only awakens a new feeling for self-reliance but also inspires to cultivate the inner being that enriches one's humane sensibilities. Which is why it serves as an eternal guide to everyone who cares for patriotism or love, peace or sympathy, conscience or peace for the entire humanity. It is interesting to refer to, in this connection, Gandhi's own interpretation of the spinning-wheel as the most appropriate symbol of non-violence and nationalism as represented through the national flag.

The spinning-wheel has its undoubted honoured place on it. The wheel on the improved pattern bereft of the spindle and the *mal,* may not be counted as a defect, if it is purely due to exigencies of art. After all, every picture had to leave something for the imagination. The spinning-wheel in a picture has no slivers with the spinners at work on it. These are left for the imagination to fill in. And this rule applies as well to the improved edition of the original flag. Thus conceived, the improvement must appear purely innocent to an unbiased mind. This tricolour flag with the wheel will certainly consist of the handspun and hand-woven *Khadi.* Our country has called it *Khadi,* whether it is woven from handspun cotton or silk. When the original conception is kept intact, no one has the right to cavil at a touch of art. We must not be deliberately inartistic. When the country was at war with a foreign power, the fact of being so engaged was in itself a work of art. Now that it has ended in success, there must be place for art, though, perhaps, of a lower type, yet quite useful, in order to perpetuate the memory of valour, such as is open to a weak nation. If any further, but not inconsistent, interpretations are added to this indispensable interpretation, then the additions will certainly be harmless. It is undoubtedly open to a rich mind to see in the same colours a subtle meaning. Unity of design lies in the diversity of colours in the whole universe. Some will recall through the wheel the name of that Prince of peace, Asoka, the founder of an empire, who ultimately gave up the pomp and the circumstances of power to become the undisputed emperor of the hearts of men, and became the representative of all the then known faiths. We would call it a legitimate interpretation of the wheel to seek in it the Wheel of Law ascribed to that living store of mercy and love.

The spinning-wheel, thus interpreted, adds to its importance in the life of billions of mankind. To liken it to and to derive it from the Asoka disc is to recognize in the insignificant-looking *Charkha* the necessity of obeying the ever-moving wheel of the Divine Law of Love.

—M.K. Gandhi: *Harijan,* 22 July 1947.

To honour the spinning-wheel by way of honouring the national flag as Gandhi highlights above is to be christened with the solemn spirit of non-violence.

To synchronize truth and non-violence is, according to Gandhi, to synchronize worship with work, and, for this end-in-view, he finds the spinning-wheel as the best means of human advancement. The wider perspective of non-violence, as he devises thus, makes room for the spinning-wheel which also encapsulates the vision that non-violence is the natural outcome of everyone enlightened with the spirit of altruism. Let everyone be happy. Let all evil forces appearing in the form of violence be encountered heroically with specific programmes of orientation both introspectively and extrospectively. The functional parameters of the spinning-wheel as Gandhi unfolds in the programmes of activities incorporate the fact that the individual must discover the inherent truth of non-violence through sincere practice. The spinning-wheel carries the core message of non-violence that stands for one's soul pure and serene. This is why Gandhi introduces it as a means worthy of making the right practice of non-violence by every individual. As he significantly observes,

> We have to make truth and non-violence not matters for mere individual practice but for practice by groups and communities and nations. That at any rate is my dream, I shall live and die in trying to realize it. My faith helps me to discover new truths every day. *Ahimsa* is the attribute of the soul, and, therefore, to be practised by everybody in all the affairs of life. If it cannot be practised in all departments, it has no practical value.
>
> — M.K. Gandhi, *Harijan,* 2 March, 1940.

Gandhi's concern with non-violence is how to infuse the spirit of fearlessness in every human being. He is well aware that fear is always the outcome of one's failure to stick to Truth and this failure on one's part is largely due to absence of self-reliance which brings forth-self-courage and self-esteem. Unless one is in a position to understand the true concept of fear, non-violence remains inoperative and devoid of its true meaning. A right exposure of non-violence demands a training of the mind through some activities which direct one to the right road to self-courage and self-esteem. Hence, the importance of introducing the spinning-wheel.

Why does the introduction of the spinning-wheel appeal to Gandhi most while he is really in the look out for the proper and most justifiable vehicle of exposition of his theory of non-violence? Why does he think that the spinning-wheel alone would pave the way to the functional glory of Truth or non-violence? The reasons are not far to seek. First, the spinning-wheel is itself the symbol of non-violence. It carries within it the spirit of freedom of mind and work. Second, the operational know-hows of the spinning-wheel demand no academic or institutional pursuit of learning. It is a natural outcome of man's needs and requirements. Third, it allows one to inculcate within oneself the spirit of non-violence in the form of accepting every challenge of life sincerely and boldly. Fourth, it teaches the prized virtue or lesson of discipline which is also an essential component of the spirit of non-violence. Fifthly, it allows one to be more interested in the enrichment of the self with a superior objective of unfolding the Divine Self, which is also the fundamental objective of non-violence.

To introduce the inherent spirit of work by means of the spinning-wheel as Gandhi does, is to introduce the inherent spirit of non-violence. Such a kind of synchronization between the spinning-wheel and non-violence is actually an accord, harmonious and disciplined, between work and worship. The labour one exerts through the spinning-wheel actually serves the fourfold purpose:

(i) It intensifies one's regular course of duties and responsibilities towards himself as well as towards others near or far.
(ii) It makes a major break-through in one's understanding of the self.
(iii) It evokes a certain sense of nationalism in its spirit of love and devotion.
(iv) It accelerates the spirit of divinity within oneself so much so that the concept of *Naranarayana* or *Satyanarayana*, love and truth in man, the Divine Being, becomes a reality.

The concept of sacrifice well nurtured in Gandhi's concept of non-violence is also at the root of his concept of the spinning-wheel. Not merely physical labour but divine labour also is the guideline of the spinning-wheel. The turning of the spinning-wheel is the steadfast turning of one's spiritual growth—the growth that ensures the efflorescence of the Divine Being. When Gandhi speaks of service to the poor by means of the spinning-wheel, he actually speaks of a non-violent crusade against poverty and wailings of the Divine self in everyone of them. A balanced harmony of relationship between man and man is, as Gandhi explicitly observes, possible through a unison of the spinning-wheel with non-violence. Citing Edwin Arnold's translation of verses from *Song Celestial,* he defends the sacrificial role of work in the form of involvement in the spinning-wheel which actually serve as a fitting exponent of his principle of non-violence.

Work is more excellent than idleness;
The body's life proceeds not, lacking work
There is a task of holiness to do,
Unlike world-binding toil, which bindeth not
The faithful soul; such earthly duty do
Free from desire, and thou shalt well perform
Thy heavenly purpose, Spake Prajapati
In the beginning, when all men were made,
And, with mankind, the sacrifice-"Do this!
Work! Sacrifice! Increase and multiply
With sacrifice! This shall be Kamadhuk,
Your 'Cow of Plenty', giving back her milk
Of all abundance. Worship the gods thereby;
The gods shall yield ye grace. Those meats ye crave
The gods will grant to Labour, when it pays
Tithes in the altar-flame. But if one eats
Fruits of the earth, rendering to kindly Heaven
No gift of toil, that thief steals from his world."
Who eat of food after their sacrifice
Are quit of fault, but they that spread a feast
All for themselves, eat sin and drink of sin.
By food the living live; food comes of rain.
And rain comes by the pious sacrifice,
And sacrifice is paid with tithes of toil;
Thus action is of Brahma, who is one,
The only, All-pervading; at all times
Present in sacrifice. He that abstains
To help the rolling wheels of this great world,
Glutting his idle sense, lives a lost life.
Shameful and vain.

Work here undoubtedly refers to physical labour, and work by way of sacrifice can only be work to be done by all for the common benefit. Such work, such sacrifice can only be spinning. I do not wish to suggest, that the author of the Divine Song had the spinning-wheel in mind. He merely laid down a fundamental principle of conduct. And reading in and applying it to India I can only think of spinning as the fittest and most acceptable sacrificial body labour. I cannot imagine anything nobler or more national than that for, say, one hour in the day, we should do all the labour that the poor must do, and thus identify ourselves with them and through them with all mankind. I cannot imagine better worship of God than that in His name I should labour for the poor even as they do. The spinning-wheel spells a more equitable distribution of the riches of the earth.

— M.K. Gandhi: *Young India,* 21 October, 1921.

To be at peace with the mind—inner as well as outer—is to be blessed with the best outcome of the spinning-wheel. Gandhi paves avenue to this peace by taking recourse to the practice with the spinning-wheel which is itself a non-violent course of action. How does it bring forth the essential outcome of non-violence? As Gandhi shows the way, it ensures the person devoted to the spinning-wheel with the following:

(i) Elimination of indolence and passivity affecting one's dynamic personality.
(ii) Loss of faith in oneself is replaced by a living and thrilling sense of optimism.
(iii) A path-breaking endeavour to unfold the self-without being a party to violence which is only a reflection of one's negative capability.
(iv) Creating a world of work anew together with an exercise of one's creative and critical thinking.
(v) A habitual exercise of detachment so forceful to negotiate the drab realities of life in a non-violent manner.
(vi) A combined endeavour of reason and intellect playing a major role in cultivation of the spirit of non-violence.

Gandhi launches the movement of the spinning-wheel among the teeming millions in our country to establish and restore eternal goodness in one and all, which is actually his end-in-view of non-violence. He is always against any temporary good by means of violence which eats up or kills one's finer humane sensibilities. Therefore, he wants to voice his protest against violence as follows:

I object to violence because when it appears to do good, the good is only temporary, the evil it does is permanent. I do not believe that the killing of even every Englishman can do the slightest good to India. The millions will be just as badly off as they are today, if someone made it possible to kill off every Englishman tomorrow. The responsibility is more ours than that of the English for the present state of things. The English will be powerless to do evil if we will but be good. Hence my incessant emphasis on reform from within.

— M.K. Gandhi, *Young India,* 21 May, 1925.

Undeniably, the spinning-wheel fulfils Gandhi's vision of 'reform from within' as a positive outcome of non-violence. It also fulfils his vision of silent social revolution by eliminating insane inward pressure of anger and ill-will which are the most poisonous fruits of violence. But goodwill and gentleness—the glorious outcome of non-violence—do not appear like a miracle. These demand continuous and sustained strivings for purity of action and perfection. Gandhi selects the spinning-wheel to exercise these potent qualities of non-violence in the simplest and most unassuming way. Moreover, in the veil of involvement in a specific kind of activity as the spinning-wheel requires, Gandhi's vision of non-violence works in it in a very objective manner. It remains beyond any personal conflict and hardly encroaches upon other belief or concepts. As such, it enjoys a world of its own well harmonized with the spirit of non-violence. What, then, are the positive outcome of the spinning-wheel in tune with the spirit of non-violence? First, the spinning-wheel itself has a world of its own when there is hardly any room for conflict and, therefore, it has an inherent appeal to encapsulate and expose the nobler visions of non-violence. Secondly, like the indomitable force of non-violence it also strengthens the person involved in the spinning programmes to reach the prized end-in-view viz., freedom of mind and dependence on the self without being a parasite. Thirdly, the sense of self-dependence also ensures the sense of self-esteem and self-glory. Naturally, it honours the invaluable components of non-violence catering to self-growth and self-development. Fourthly, the spinning-wheel teaches the lesson of baptising others as one's very own irrespective of power, position or glory—a quality that Gandhi highlights in his theory of non-violence.

Admittedly, the spinning-wheel is, as it were, the other side of the coin of non-violence bearing the same value of self-development through self-activity without plunging oneself into the world of conflict, destruction or hatred. Love serves as the guiding force in his philosophy of non-violence as well as at that of the spinning-wheel. Gandhi ensured the fact that with love as the guiding force, other forces become inoperative and transitory. As the spinning-wheel creates a newer world of self-awareness, the breeding ground of hatred or violence gradually becomes infertile. Which is why it paves path to newer strategies positive as well as healthy and, therefore, beneficial to create a world blessed with the spirit of love or non-violence.

At the backdrop of the philosophy of the spinning-wheel, the following components which represents the essence of non-violence are always existent and operative:

(1) Non-violence is the law of the human race and is infinitely greater than and superior to brute force.
(2) In the last resort it does not avail to those who do not possess a living faith in the God of love.
(3) Non-violence affords the fullest protection to one's self-respect and sense of honour, but not always to possession of land or movable property, though its habitual practice does prove a better bulwark than the possession of armed men to defend them. Non-violence in the very nature of things is of no assistance in the defence of ill-gotten gains and immoral acts.
(4) Individuals and nations who would practise non-violence must be prepared to sacrifice (nations to the last man) their all except honour. It is, therefore, inconsistent with the possession of other people's countries, i.e., modern imperialism which is frankly based on force for its defence.
(5) Non-violence is a power which can be wielded equally by all —children, young men and women or grown up people, provided they have a living faith in the God of Love and have therefore equal love for all mankind. When non-violence is accepted as the law of life it must pervade the whole being and not be applied to isolated acts.
(6) It is a profound error to suppose that whilst the law is good enough for individuals it is not for masses of mankind.

— M.K. Gandhi, *Harijan,* 5 September, 1936.

Gandhi bases his philosophy of the spinning-wheel on the principles of non-violence because he thinks that it is the best way to negotiate the idle mind with workforce ill-directed towards passivity and spirit motivated to serve violence or defeat. He has keenly observed the role of disastrous alien forces eating up the inherent vitality or potentiality of mankind. Moreover, he also aches with the gradual erosion of self-esteem and self-reliance. With such a continual erosion of consciousness, man loses his finer feelings and sentiments, loses his indomitable strength of mind and seeks shelter in utter cowardice. Gandhi's main concern is to emancipate man from cowardice and violence. His primary objective is to allow man to manifest his inner strength that is nourished in non-violence. In order to do so man must know himself by acting himself.

He must react to his own position of peril in violence and utter submission to violent opponents. Hence, the importance of the spinning-wheel. It is a positive challenge against violence. As such, it preaches and teaches the lesson of learning how to be a winner in the battle of self-defence. It equips one with the weapon of life anew to negotiate violence not by violence but by non-violence. The inherent force of the spinning-wheel is, indeed, the force of non-violence which teaches the lesson of how to die in order to know how to live by translating the invaluable qualities of self-honour and self-reliance in particular. It is an irony that such a lesson of learning how to be as one should be in the context of untoward forces has yet to receive proper attention. The appalling ruin of cottage industry signalling the ruin of the valiant mind to face all constraints is a veritable symptom of cowardice inviting enemies of violence or untoward forces to plunder rich indigenous resources. What a meek submission at the cost of ingenuity and strength of mind that should never yield to violence in any form whatsoever! One might recall in this connection Gandhi's strong reaction to the role of meek people embracing dishonour and violence:

> The people of a village near Bettiah told me that they had run away whilst the police were looting their houses and molesting their womenfolk. When they said that they had run away because I had told them to be non-violent, I hung my head in shame. I assured them that such was not the meaning of my non-violence. I expected them to intercept the mightiest power that might be in the act of harming those who were under their protection, and draw without retaliation all harm upon their own heads even to the point of death, but never to run away from the storm centre. It was manly enough to defend one's property, honour or religion at the point of the sword. It was manlier and nobler to defend them without seeking to injure the wrongdoer. But it is unmanly, unnatural and dishonourable to forsake the post of duty and, in order to save one's skin, to leave property, honour or religion to the mercy of the wrongdoer. I could see my way of delivering the message of *Ahimsa* to those who knew how to die, not to those who were afraid of death.
>
> —Mahadev Desai: *Gandhiji in Indian Villages,* S. Ganesan, Madras, 1927, p. 254.

To helplessly ape western industrial models and thereby kill the life of the spinning-wheel is to kill the potent force of protest and run away from *Kurukshetra*. This is an utter shame in the form of submission to the violent forces in cowardice and betrays the Gandhian philosophy of non-violence almost in the same manner as above. Our unmanliness in facing all eventualities which stand in the way of our proper approach to the spinning-wheel should be dealt with the teaching of non-violence as Gandhi advocates:

> He is no follower of *Ahimsa* who does not care a straw if he kills a man by inches by deceiving him in trade, or who would protect by force of arms a few cows and make away with the butcher or who, in order to do a supposed good to his country, does not mind killing off a few officials. All these are actuated by hatred, cowardice and fear. Here the love of the cow or the country is a vague thing intended to satisfy one's vanity or soothe a stinging conscience.
>
> *Ahimsa*, truly understood, is in my humble opinion a panacea for all evils mundane and extra-mundane. We can never overdo it. Just at present we are not doing it at all. *Ahimsa* does not displace the practice of other virtues, but renders their practice imperatively necessary before it can be practised even in its rudiments.
>
> —M.K. Gandhi: *Speeches and Writings of Mahatma Gandhi,* G.A. Natesan & Company, Madras, 1934.

Deep in his heart of hearts, Gandhi feels that the spinning-wheel necessitates incorporation in the day-to-day affairs of the Indian life and society, the spirit of self-service because this will specifically dispel the disbelief of Swaraj through non-violence. Mere sentimentalism exhibited through violent action or revolution will definitely breed hatred and narrowness of mind. Moreover, with involvement in violence in any form whatsoever, the finer visions of love and co-operation are terribly shattered. The two Great Wars are sufficient for instilling the germs of hatred amongst mankind. Violence in place of non-violence and war in place of peace are the common and inevitable offshoots of disbelief and misunderstanding which erupt all finer sentiments and nobler visions of the ascent of man by means of a common endeavour. In fact, the spinning-wheel serves this purpose of some sort of a viable joint and communicated enterprise between man and man so that the sense of disbelief or of destruction to life and property does not at any cost take the upper hand. The spirit of non-violence as the inherent guiding force of the spinning-wheel makes everyone aware that violence must be answered by a positive force—a force that never allows annihilation of mankind.

The bridge that the spinning-wheel creates between the two antagonistic forces of violence and non-violence is that of love in course of continual and sustained work elevated to the ardent platform of worship.

The spirit of love that Gandhi wants to introduce by means of the spinning-wheel is actually an inherent spirit of love as non-violence stands for. All arguments, all theories, all visions of life are inseparable from the spirit of non-violence, and so, when he launches the movement of the spinning-wheel, he actually launches the movement of non-violence in the form of practice in the art of love for countrymen. Through 'common productive work' as it aims at, it exercises the art of love so valuable for patriotic fervour and national unity. As Gandhi observes,

> The spinning-wheel is not meant to oust a single man or woman from his or her occupation. It seeks only to harness every single idle minute of our millions for 'common productive work.'
>
> —M.K. Gandhi: *Young India,* 23 January, 1930.

A symbol of *national prosperity* and *freedom,* the spinning-wheel makes inroads in the heart of everyone the spirit of love as inherent in the spirit of non-violence. It allows everyone to testify the real nature of his love which is nothing but Truth, and Truth and non-violence are, as Gandhi categorically observes, one and the same. What sort of Truth does the spinning-wheel reveal? It is that sort of Truth that works in everyone's mind to know his real identity—the identity of man as man. Non-violence as Gandhi preaches and practises, also reveals the Truth working in everyone's mind for identification of the true self, the true being. From this point of view, both the spirit of the spinning-wheel and the spirit of non-violence are one and the same.

Gandhi's vision of *Swaraj* by non-violence is a vision of positive approach to life and work. It is a vision well nourished and supplemented by the constructive approach to life and work for which the spinning-wheel stands. The end-in-view of self-rule or self-control can only be achieved by means of a non-violent strategy and the spirit of self-rule or self-control should be ignited by self-esteem and self-activity. Gandhi enkindles that spirit among the masses by introducing the spinning-wheel which has actually made a silent but strong and effective revolution in this respect. A slow but steady effort at an awakening of national consciousness by means of non-violence as the spinning-wheel reflects, is what he continually urges:

> I contend that the revolutionary method cannot succeed in India. If an open warfare were a possibility, I may concede that we may

> tread the path of violence that the other countries have and at least evolve the qualities that bravery on the battlefield brings forth. But the attainment of *Swaraj* through warfare I hold an impossibility for any time that we can foresee. Warfare may give us another rule for the English rule, but not self-rule in terms of the masses. The pilgrimage to *Swaraj* is a painful climb. It requires attention to details. It means vast organizing ability, it means penetration into the villages solely for the service of the villagers. In other words, it means national education i.e. education of the masses. It will not spring like the magician's mango. It will grew almost unperceived like the banian tree. A bloody revolution will never perform the trick.
>
> —M.K. Gandhi: *Young India,* 21 May, 1925.

To awaken the inherent strength and dignity of man by the spinning-wheel is to awaken the spirit of non-violence. As the latter teaches the lesson of fearlessness, the former actually shows how to learn that lesson by means of sincere and devoted practice. That is non-cooperation as a positive component of non-violence. That is the spirit of the spinning-wheel also. That is the way to do justice to the soul within. When Gandhi speaks of non-cooperation as an effective tool of non-violence to safeguard the soul within, he also speaks of the spinning-wheel as the latter prepares everyone to wage a silent revolution against violence all the time polluting the soul within. In explaining non-cooperation Gandhi hints at the intrinsic spirit of the spinning-wheel, which saves the soul within:

> Non-co-operation is an attempt to awaken the masses to a sense of their dignity and power. This can only be by enabling them to realize that they need not fear brute force, if they would but know the soul within.
>
> —M.K. Gandhi: *Young India,* 1 December, 1920.

To understand and appreciate non-violence as an active force, Gandhi introduces the spinning-wheel in such a manner as to realize non-violence as a Truth-force or soul-force. This is why the spinning-wheel epitomizes the essence of non-violence i.e. the active involvement of every individual to understand and intensify the power of the All Serene within. The only point to be remembered in this connection is that the spinning-wheel acts as a subtle force of non-violence and anything expected of it acting like a magic would be a travesty to non-violence.

Therefore, the guiding spirit of introducing the spinning-wheel should always be that of non-violence as ordained by Gandhi in a very significant manner:

> Non-violence is an active force of the highest order. It is soul-force or the power of Godhead within us. Imperfect man cannot grasp the whole of that essence—he would not be able to bear its full blaze, but even an infinitesimal fraction of it, when it becomes active within us, can work wonders. The sun in the heaven fills the whole universe with its life-giving warmth. But if one went too near it, it would consume him to ashes. Even so it is with Godhead. We become Godlike to the extent we realize non-violence; but we can never become wholly God. Non-violence is like radium in its action. An infinitesimal quantity of it embedded in a malignant growth, acts continuously, silently and ceaselessly till it has transformed the whole mass of the diseased tissue into a healthy one. Similarly, even a little of true non-violence acts in a silent, subtle, unseen way and leavens the whole society.
>
> —M.K. Gandhi: *Harijan,* 12 November, 1938.

When would we revitalize the inner spirit of the spinning-wheel in terms of that of non-violence as above?

5

RELIGION AND THE SPINNING-WHEEL
Gandhian Introspection

I give you the end of a golden string
Only wind it into a ball,
It will lead you in at Heaven's gate
Built in Jerusalem's wall.

— William Blake

IN ELUCIDATING the prophetic vision of Mahatma Gandhi on his seventy-seventh birthday, 2 October, 1946, Lady Pathick Lawrence quotes the lines as above from William Blake and heightens the glory of the spinning-wheel as a great religious force. In fact, it is a divine symbol and means of identification with millions of people in all walks of life. As Gandhi never accepts any God *sans* the dumb millions who are his only mouthpiece, the spinning-wheel cannot but be a fitting symbol to identify oneself with one's own inherent divine spirit.

To Gandhi, religion is always an experience—individual or group—intense, soul-searching, full of Truth or non-violence and divinely humanistic or vice-versa. It is an experience creative as well as constructive to march for excellence beyond excellence. The wheel of life is as it were the wheel of spinning always aiming at perfection from all humanistic and divine points of view. Hence, the importance of purity as the most important component for the spinning-wheel as a characteristic tool for self-service and self-assessment. It also lessens the confusion of religion because it combines within itself work and worship.

The spirit of purity and simplicity that the spinning-wheel allows us to exercise is itself an invaluable component of religion in practice.

Gandhi wants to introduce the spinning-wheel as a remover of factionalism or hatred by means of constructive work and non-violence. This alone would go a long way in dispelling the darkness of irreligion. Elucidating its role as a symbol of non-violence by highlighting self-purification in the exercise of simplicity and purity as components of religion, he observes:

> How does it (the spinning-wheel) become the symbol of non-violence? As I have already explained, the essential thing is the spirit in which you regard it, the attribute you invest it with. It is no quinine pill which has certain inherent properties in it, apart from what you think about it. The spinning-wheel has no such inherent property. Take the *Gayatri Mantra.* It cannot have the same effect on the non-Hindus as it has on me, nor can the *Kalma* have the same reaction on me as it has on the Muslims. Even so the spinning-wheel in itself has nothing which can teach *Ahimsa* or bring *Swaraj.* But you have to think it with those attributes and it is transformed. Its obvious value is the service of the poor, but that does not necessarily mean that it should be a symbol of non-violence or an indispensable condition for *Swaraj.* But we since 1920 have connected the wheel with *Swaraj* and non-violence.
>
> —D.G. Tendulkar: *Mahatma,* Publications Division, Ministry of Information and Broadcasting, Government of India, 1969, Vol. V, pp. 95-96.

To instil the true concept of religion by means of the spinning-wheel, Gandhi advocates *Sarvadharmasamanatva.* This allows the practical world of the spinning-wheel to be more generous and flexible than scriptures or religious books as an approach. The cathedral of religion that it represents, allows entry of everyone interested in honouring everyone. The symbol of simplicity is itself a religious course *par excellence,* which allows extinction of the little self and encounters with the Divine Self.

It is interesting to note in this connection how Gandhi upholds the spirit of the spinning-wheel in terms of religion and keeps it apart from petty interests like national independence or national prosperity as it is normally envisaged. He always sticks to the introspective end-in-view of the spinning-wheel as the fitting vehicle of awakening and respecting the 'Kingdom of God' within each and every person. Otherwise, the search for freedom becomes meaningless and in that case he would always remain aloof from launching the movement through the spinning-wheel. Explaining his constructive programme by means of highlighting the introspective vision of the spinning-wheel in terms of awakening the 'Kingdom of God' within everyone, he remarks:

> I am as impatient as any of you to reach our goal, but I realize that the task is an uphill one. India has been enslaved for so long, that it has killed all initiative and originally in us and it has filled us with the paralysis of despair. The constructive work cannot make headway without a resuscitation of these lost qualities in us and the attainment of independence through non-violence and truth must ramain an empty dream unless the constructive work can be carried through to success. Freedom is bound to come. It is coming. But mere political freedom will not satisfy me. It will certainly not satisfy the world, which expects much bigger things from India. The independence of my conception means nothing less than the realization of the 'Kingdom of God within you' and on this earth. I would rather work for and die in the pursuit of this dream, though it may never be realized. It means infinite patience and perseverance. If India is satisfied with the mere attainment of political independence and there is nothing better for me to do, then you will find me retiring to the Himalayas, leaving those who wish to listen to me to seek me out there.
>
> —D.G. Tendulkar: *Mahatma,* Publications, Division, Ministry of Information and Broadcasting, Government of India, 1969, Vol. VI, p. 307.

The introspective vision of religion that Gandhi advocates through the spinning-wheel is the vision of a living image—an image that is both serene and constructive. This is why he emphasizes on seriousness of purpose in restoring and enriching a living faith in the spinning-wheel. There must, within it, a combination of the head and the heart, emotion and intellect. Otherwise, the end-in-view of synchronizing work with worship will be terribly jeopardised. As a symbol of non-violence which is in itself a symbol of religion in the true sense of the term, it always necessitates an endearing and sincere approach. Gandhi spells out this necessity by referring to the story of Ekalavya in the *Mahabharata:*

> We Charkha-pliers are regarded as a dense-lot, and indeed we should deserve the description if we ply it unintelligently. Remember the story of Ekalavya in the *Mahabharata,* who made a

> clay image of Drona and sat opposite to it worshipping in order to achieve accomplishment in archery. For him it was no clay image. It was a living image and so his faith was rewarded. We should all have the faith of Ekalavya. And if we could have that faith in the *Charkha,* it would be a living image for us. And then we would bring to bear on it all our intellect and our will and heart.
>
> — *Ibid.*, p. 160.

Gandhi's primary concern with the spinning-wheel is, therefore, how to honour it as the religion of one's very own—the religion that characteristically responds to the inner voice. In fact, the world awaits revival of the inner voice which has the supreme authority in the life of every human being. As for himself, Gandhi strengthens the role of the inner voice as it waits for 'a long and severe course of training', where the spinning-wheel shines forth very significantly. In claiming the supreme authority of his own inner voice crystallized in long and severe course of training in the spinning-wheel, he categorically observes:

> Nobody has to my knowledge questioned the possibility of the inner voice speaking to some, and it is a gain to the world even if one person's claim to speak under the authority of the inner voice can be really sustained. Many may make the claim, but not all will be able to substantiate it. But it cannot and ought not to be suppressed for the sake of preventing false claimants. There is no danger whatsoever if many people could truthfully represent the inner voice. But, unfortunately, there is no remedy against hypocrisy. Virtue must not be suppressed because many will feign it. Men have always been found throughout the world cliaming to speak for the inner voice. But no harm has yet overtaken the world through their shortlived activities. Before one is able to listen to that voice, one has to go through a long and fairly severe course of training, and when it is the inner voice that speaks, it is unmistakable. The world cannot be successfully fooled for all time. There is, therefore, no danger of anarchy setting in because a humble man like me will not be suppressed and will dare to claim the authority of the inner voice, when he believes that he has heard it.
>
> — M.K. Gandhi: *Harijan,* 18 March, 1933.

Admittedly, Gandhi's concern is to show how the spinning-wheel shatters all form of hypocrisy in denying the 'Kingdom of God' within everyone. A firm faith in the spinning-wheel is to have a firm faith in the All Serene. Unless one realizes as a *Karmayogi* the inner response one receives from the spinning-wheel, the purpose of the latter is to a great extent defeated. Gandhi of course, goes a step further in identifying and analysing the role of the spinning-wheel as an exponent of true religion. He visualizes God in the spinning-wheel, experiences religion in work and practises a communion with the Divine Spirit of mankind through it. In his own words,

> For me the spinning-wheel is all in all. I do not know whether I am a *Karmayogi* or any other *Yogi.* I know that I cannot live without work. I crave to die with my hand at the spinning-wheel. If one has to establish communion with God through some means, why not through the spinning-wheel? Him who worships Me, says the Lord in the *Gita,* I guide along the right path and see to his needs. My God is myriad-formed. And while sometimes I see Him in the spinning-wheel, at other times I see Him in communal unity, then again in the removal of untouchability; and that is how I establish communion with Him according as the spirit moves me.
>
> —D.G. Tendulkar: *Mahatma,* Publications Division, Ministry of Information and Broadcasting, Government of India, 1969, Vol. IV, p. 162.

To harmonize the inner and the outer needs of the toiling masses exposed to poverty and starvation by means of the spinning-wheel, Gandhi extends the vision of religion like synchronizing it with communal harmony or removal of untouchability and honours the role of the spinning-wheel as a religio-economic force for regeneration of mankind. His concern with the spinning-wheel, therefore, rests on the educated community not as an economic force of reorientation of society but as a purely spiritual force directly. But in case of the economically frustrated masses, it is primarily an economic force bringing forth the essence of religion through worship in work. In fact, Gandhi gives an altogether new dimension of spiritualism or religion in its finer essence by means of launching the movement of the spinning-wheel as an indispensable tool for revitalization of man and society. The source point of religion or of spiritualism is the initial assurance of 'barest living' as he has mentioned earlier, and the spinning-wheel translates that assurance into reality in the quickest possible way. Moreover, as it has neither any conflict nor any competition with the normal procedures of exercising economic stability or religion, it appeals to human endeavour in the simplest and most dignified manner. This is why the spinning-wheel is endearing both to the educated and to the poor and ones bereft of the blessings of education. As Gandhi clarifies the point of its actual role in this context:

> Before the educated classes, I do not place the economic aspect of the spinning-wheel. I simply want them to realize the spiritual aspect of the thing. By spinning and wearing *Khadi* alone, they will express their sympathy for the poor. But for the poor the economic is the spiritual. You cannot make any other appeal to those starving millions.
>
> —M.K. Gandhi: *Young India,* 5 May, 1927.

Gandhi rightly reminds us of the fact that the spinning-wheel is the surest means of eliminating superstitions and prejudices. It must play its vital role in national awakening which will voice the religious regeneration of mankind in its truest perspective. He urges on liberal financial investment to disseminate the spirit of the spinning-wheel which brings religion to man in the forms of practice in self-reliance, goodness and greatness. The boycott of foreign cloth by endearing the *Khadi*—a boon of the spinning-wheel in the forms of self-labour and self-reliance—is the boycott of being self-paralysed without caring for self-dignity and the dignity of the nation as a whole. In elucidating his religion of self-service for national dignity and national reawakening by means of introducing the spinning-wheel in every home. Gandhi observes:

> *Swadeshi* propaganda in its intensive and exclusive form had to come and it has come in its order. It was, and is, part in the non-cooperation programme. It is, I claim, the biggest, the safest, and the surest part. It could not be taken up earlier in its present form. The country had to see its way clear to the spinning-wheel. It has to be purged of the old superstitions and prejudices. The country had to appreciate the futility of the boycott of the British goods merely, and equally of all foreign goods. It had to see that it lost its liberty by giving up *Swadeshi* in cloth and that it could regain it by reverting to hand-spun and hand-woven cloth. It had to see that it lost its artistic taste and talent, when it innocently ceased to spin and weave by the hand. It had to see that it was not even so much the military drain, as the loss of this supplementary industry that sapped India's vitality and made famines as ever-recurring event in Indian life. Men with faith in the spinning-wheel had to rise in every province, and people had to appreciate the beauty and the

use of *Khaddar.*

— M.K. Gandhi: *Young India,* 13 April, 1921.

Gandhi is well aware of the role of women in disseminating the inner spirit of the spinning-wheel—the spirit of the religion of self-enrichment through self-labour—and keeping a high profile of national advancement. In one of his addresses to women he appeals:

> I have not known a mother throwing away her baby even though it may appear ugly to an outsider. So should it be with the patriotic women of India about Indian manufactures. And for you only hand-spun and hand-woven can be regarded as Indian manufactures. During the transition stage you can get only coarse *Khadi* in abundance. You may add all the arts to it that your taste allows or requires. And if you will be satisfied with coarse *Khadi* for a few months, India need not despair of seeing a revival of the fine, rich and coloured *old garments* which were once the envy and despair of the world. I assure you that a six months' course of self-denial will show you that what we today regard as artistic is only falsely so, and that true art takes note not merely of form but also of what lies behind. There is an art that kills and an art that gives life. The fine fabric that we have imported from the West or the Far East has literally killed millions of our brothers and sisters, and delivered thousands of our dear sisters to a life of shame. True art must be evidence of happiness, contentment and purity of its authors. And if you will have such art revived in our midst, the use of *Khadi* is obligatory on the best of you at the present moment.
>
> —D.G. Tendulkar: *Mahatma,* Publications Division, Ministry of Information and Broadcasting, Government of India, 1969, Vol. II, pp. 56-57.

Gandhi further intensifies the role of women in involving themselves directly with the spinning-wheel and by doing so, disseminate the true religion of rebuilding every future citizen of India brave, simple and God-fearing:

> The main burden of spinning must, as of old, fall on your shoulders. Two hundred years ago, the women of India spun not only for home demand but also for foreign lands. They spun not merely coarse counts but the finest that the world has ever spun. No machine has yet reached the fineness of the yarn spun by our ancestors. If we are to cope with the demand for *Khadi* during the

two months and afterwards, you must form the spinning clubs, institute spinning competitions and flood the Indian market with hand-spun yarn. For this purpose some of you have to become experts in spinning, carding and adjusting the spinning-wheels. This means ceaseless toil. You will not look upon spinning as a means of livelihood. For the middle class it should supplement the income of the family, and for poor women, it is undoubtedly a means of livelihood. The spinning-wheel should be, as it was, the widow's loving companion.

The economic and the moral salvation of India thus rests mainly with you. The future of India lies on your knees, for you will nurture the future generation. You can bring up the children of India to become simple godfearing and brave men and women, or you can coddle them to be weaklings unfit to brave the storms of life and used to foreign fineries which they would find it difficult in after life to discard.

— D.G. Tendulkar: *Mahatma,* Publications Division, Ministry of Information and Broadcasting, Government of India, 1969, Vol. II, p. 37.

The religion of simplicity as Gandhi intends to be exercised at all cost and disseminated in right earnest is the only religion of man endearing man in spite of numerous points of disagreements. And, for this religion of simplicity, he finds the spinning-wheel as the best exponent of whatever brings forth goodness out of simplicity.

Again, to translate 'purity of character in action' Gandhi urges for devotion to the spinning-wheel. Such a devotion would enable one to encounter *Daridranarayan,* the All Serene embodied in the poor in the most sacred manner. In his address to the students of the Benaras Hindu University in 1930, he advises.

If you will express the requisite purity of character in action, you cannot do it better than through the spinning-wheel. Of all the myriads of God, *Daridranarayan* is the most sacred, in as much as it represents the untold millions of the poor people as distinguished from the few rich people. The easiest and the best way of identifying yourselves somewhat with these starving millions is to spread the message of the spinning-wheel in the threefold manner suggested by me. You can spread it by becoming expert spinners, by wearing *Khadi* and by pecuniary contributions.

—*Ibid.,* p. 377.

As an ardent follower of the religion of Buddha, Gandhi emphasizes on the religious principle that it is a sin to pass a single moment in idleness. Hence, his insistence on utilizing every idle moment in the devotion to the spinning-wheel that saves him from being sinned against God. The cultural aspect of the spinning-wheel as it is reflected through exercise of incomparable simplicity is closely related to this religion of work as worship. To invite national catastrophe by encouraging alien tinsel splendour—a schizophrenic habit which has even now its terrible overpowering role amidst ourselves—is to allow this religion to be polluted or to be extinct. As a foreseer of cultural peril Gandhi sticks to the spinning-wheel primarily to make us aware of the fact that it is better to remain unaffluent through the culture of the spinning-wheel than to be puffed up with vain pride in apeing alien culture because that would be killing oneself by dishonouring one's own cultural identity and heritage which is actually the mouthpiece of one's religion.

Again, to be devoted to the spinning-wheel is to be justified to the religion of sympathy and care for the members living in and around us. This is what may be described as conjoint communicated religion by means of involvement in indigenous work. A living contact with people from all walks of life can be most beautifully made through the spinning-wheel by delivering the artistic but simple products made of hand-spun yarn. And the religion of fostering at one's own spirit of service towards others is also exercised in the most ardent manner. The practical experience of service towards *Daridranarayan* as Gandhi highlights in his concept of religion by means of the spinning-wheel becomes a living and thrilling reality.

Gandhi wants to introduce the spinning-wheel as the mouthpiece of *Daridranarayan,* where the role it plays is one of preparation for and untiring devotion to self-sacrifice. In fact, the religion of the spinning-wheel speaks of the 'economics of God', which is always devoted to strengthening the indomitable spirit of man to eliminate the 'economics of the Devil'. Gandhi superbly deals with this religious vision of the spinning-wheel in one of his speeches delivered before the temple of Harihar at Davangere, Mysore in August 1927:

> It is said that if God made man in His image, man made God in his own, and it is no wonder that what we see in our temples, at the present day, are lifeless images of us, the lifeless devotees. If we would make them living images of God, we must transform our lives, we must end our communal squabbles, and we must befriend the suppressed, and live pure lives. Hari is the Protector in the

> Hindu Trinity, and Hara is the Destroyer. When God finds that the rich oppress the poor, instead of taking them under their protecting wings. He then assumes His fearful aspect of Hara, and deals destruction all around. When the rich and the poor identify themselves with one another, then will Hari and Hara unite, and it is my ambition to establish a real living image of Harihareshvara by presenting a *Charkha* to the country. The *Charkha* is the symbol of sacrifice, and sacrifice is essential for the establishment of the image of the deity.
>
> —*Ibid.*, p. 277.

To adore Harihareshvara by means of devotion to the spinning-wheel as Gandhi earnestly appeals, is to give religion a dynamic avenue of afflorescence in every individual. It is the easiest way to understand and appreciate self-honour which is actually to honour the Divine Being within oneself. Again, as it is purely practical in approach, it allows transcendence of religion in the most undisturbed and effective manner. There is neither any room for dogmatism or obscuranticism nor is there any uncontroiled arena of slipshod liberalism. Gandhi introduces a disciplined approach to practice in the spinning-wheel even for those who are master spinners and weavers and this adherence to discipline will boosts the purity of performance as well as of perfection in true religious poignance and devotion.

Gandhi synchronizes religion as above with the spinning-wheel by making inroads to inner awareness. While discussing standardization in connection with *Khaddar,* he unfolds the truth that it appeals to 'the heart and then to the eye'. Therefore, a change in approach to the spinning-wheel which has its role of inwardness through an appeal to the heart by its product as *Khaddar* is, far surpasses the importance of its orientation or modernization in the undesirable process of bleaching. A real and worthwhile penetration into the life of every spinner would not only bring about a radical change in life style but would also baptise him with the religion of love, self-esteem and honesty. As Gandhi elaborately explains:

> A poor ordinary spinner cannot always spin thread of a uniform quality. She is not a machine. Today she may be unwell, tomorrow her child may be ill and her mind will be distracted. If you have love for the poor spinner or for her child, you will not insist on having smooth, even thread always, but be satisfied with what she can give, so long as she gives her best in the condition in which she finds herself at the moment. The sacred touch of her hand

gives life and history of *Khadi* which the machine-made yarn can never give. The art that is in the machine-made article, appeals only to the eye, the art in *Khadi* appeals first to the heart and then to the eye. I would, therefore, deprecate the bleaching of *Khadi.* It adds to the cost of production, affects the durability of cloth and makes the detection of fraud ever so much difficult. We must not pamper the popular fancy, but seek to cultivate a new taste. A few washes in the ordinary course will suffice to make *Khadi* perfectly white and give it a softness which bleaching destroys. We must make everybody contribute his or her mite to reduce all unnecessary cost.

* * * * *

The rules governing the reduction of the price of *Khadi* are somewhat, if not wholly, different from those that apply to purely commercial articles, produced chiefly for profit. In *Khadi,* there is a limitation to the improvement of tools. But there is no limitation to the improvement of human honesty and intelligence. If we despair of these two, then we must despair of *Khadi.*

— D.G. Tendulkar: *Mahatma,* Publications Division, Ministry of Information and Broadcasting, Government of India, 1969, Vol. III, pp. 292-293.

To be justified to one's divine self is to devote to truth and love by means of service to oneself as well as to others. Gandhi allows the freedom of service in order to arrive at this aim in the most natural and habitual way. The spinning-wheel is undeniably an ideal means or tool to be in tune with this objective, and this works most effectively because the inward feelings of true religion are best manifested in sincere involvement with it.

Gandhi prefers the spinning-wheel as the most prominent vehicle of living religion because it responds most vitally to the inward sensibilities of every person. The components that lie unused or dormant in the mind of man e.g. sympathy, self-service, self-dependence, self-respect etc. find a functional avenue with creative consciousness. These become vibrant exponents of living religion as these endear the most potent force of every religion that the Temple of God is there in every human being and it is the duty and responsibility of every human being to continually exert himself towards enrichment and manifestation of the living spirit of this Temple. The spinning-wheel is the wheel of such an involvement where everyone finds an avenue to look at himself inwardly and look anew with the divine spirit already in him. The blessings of religion are derived only when that manifestation of the inward vision has its bearings upon others in all walks of life. Moreover, the religion thus practised by means of the spinning-wheel becomes ever abiding, all pervasive and universal.

To endear the spinning-wheel as the mouthpiece of living religion is what Gandhi time and again refers in course of dispelling all doubts associated with it. He advises the volunteers and particularly the students to follow it like a sacrament while accepting its role in bringing about a definite change in the lives of the masses. Reacting to a statement that it has no fun in it, he observes:

> You say there is no fun in spinning. But I ask you, is there any fun in reciting the *Gayatri?* Is there any fun in reciting the *Kalma?* You do it as it is a duty, as it is a sacrament. India is dying. She is on death-bed. Have you ever watched a dying man? Have you ever felt his feet? You find that they are cold and benumbed, though you still feel some warmth on the head and comfort yourselves that the life is not yet gone out of him. But it is ebbing away. Even so the masses of India —the feet of the Mother—are cold and palsied. If you want to save India, do it by doing little that I ask for. I warn you. Take up the wheel betimes or perish.
>
> —D.G. Tendulkar: *Mahatma,* Publications Division, Ministry of Information and Broadcasting, Government of India, 1969, Vol. II, p. 191.

What emerges from the above address by Gandhi is that he is always in favour of a new religion that teaches how to safeguard and enrich self-respect and self-development of each individual in order to safeguard and enrich national honour and national development. In an earlier statement he defines national education in terms of the spinning-wheel which also unfolds and disseminates the new religion of humanism. As he advises the students:

> That education is national which educates in you a sense of fellow-feeling for all your countrymen, which teaches you to melt at the woes of your countrymen. And nothing is so universally useful as the spinning-wheel
>
> —*Ibid.,* p. 185.

Whither national education, whither the religion of humanism, whither the spinning-wheel for that end-in-view at present or in the century ahead?

6

HUMANISM AND THE SPINNING-WHEEL
Gandhian Forethoughts

THE SPINNING-WHEEL is the true symbol of humanism. It is the life-blood of man teaching him the lesson of self-respect—the lesson that bears one of the most essential components of the humanistic spirit. This spirit very often lying dormant demands a boost, a spurt, an ignition either directly or indirectly. The spinning-wheel is, indeed, an effective vehicle to serve as a spurt in man both inwardly and outwardly, directly and indirectly. It acts directly when it delivers the dormant human spirit to act according to its own judicious vision of self-growth and self-development. It acts indirectly when there is an initial response by man to a routinised activity, a certain form of habitual involvement in work that orients him towards his own goodness first and at the same time the goodness of one and all.

A humanist *par excellence,* Gandhi introduces the spinning-wheel with the basic forethoughts of humanism as identified above. His main concern in this respect is to foster the spirit of humanism by introducing the spinning-wheel as the only effective means of establishing a global non-violent society. The march for advancement of humanism, as he spells out, depends on how we accelerate our march through the spinning-wheel. With this objective in view, he criticizes the role of the Spinners' Association upon whom he banks considerably. A highly centralised organisation as it is, it has failed to highlight the non-violent spirit of the spinning-wheel, and instead, dehumanized it as a mere tool for production of *Khadi* to alleviate economic sufferings. In his own words,

> I had hoped that through it the message could penetrate to every village and every home in our country and that thereby we would

> be able to show to the world how a non-violent society could be built on the basis of the spinning-wheel. But *** leave alone every home, the wheel has not yet even reached every village. *** If it had been able to penetrate to the seven lakhs of villages, no power on earth could have crushed it. Government cannot send crores of men and women to jail nor can it mow down all this humanity by machine guns. Even if they killed one crore out of forty crores, they could not have stopped our onward march to our goal. Indeed the speed of our march would have been accelerated.
>
> — M.K. Gandhi: *Swaraj Through Charkha,* compiled by Kanu Gandhi, All India Spinners' Association, Sevagram, 1945.

The concept of true *Swadeshi* as Gandhi interprets through the spinning-wheel is the concept of true humanism. He does not allow discrimination in the welfare of one nation by means of the spinning-wheel between alien and indigenous assistance if it is directed towards the goodness of everyone. The false interpretation of *Swadeshi* nursled in alien aid even though controlled indigenously has necessitated him to define and explain *Swadeshi* as follows:

> If I have to use the adjective 'true' before *Swadeshi,* a critic may well ask, "Is there also false *Swadeshi?'* Unfortunately I have to answer 'Yes'. As since the days of *Khadi,* I am supposed to be an authority on *Swadeshi,* numerous conundrums are presented to me by correspondents. And I have been obliged to distinguish between the two kinds of *Swadeshi.* If foreign capital is mixed with indigenous, or if foreign talent is mixed with indigenous, is the enterprise *Swadeshi?* There are other questions too. But I had better reproduced the definition I gave to a Minister the other day. "Any article is *Swadeshi* if it subserves the interest of the millions, even though the capital and talent are foreign but under effective Indian control." Thus *Khadi* of the definition of the A.I.S.A. would be true *Swadeshi* even though the capital may be all foreign and there may be Western specialists employed by the Indian Board. *** For in the A.I.S.A. the capital is all indigenous and the whole of the talent also. But I would love to secure the engineering talent of the West to give me a village wheel which will beat the existing wheels, though deep down in me. I have the belief that the improvements that indigenous talent has made are by no means to be despised.
>
> — M.K. Gandhi: *Harijan,* 25 February, 1939.

The liberal form of humanism that Gandhi extends towards improvement of the spinning-wheel shows his rare vision of the future. In fact, his experiments with the spinning-wheel has its close relation with what man is and what man should be in the endless adventure of human progress.

How does Gandhi visualize the spinning-wheel from the point of humanism? What lesson does he actually want to infuse among mankind? How does he unfold the inwardness of the spinning-wheel which itself stands for the essence of humanism? As Gandhi significantly answers:

> The music of the *Charkha* murmurs sweetly, that we are all one, born to be equal sharers in the goods of the earth, with no one higher or wealthier than the other. Yet the world is today full of inequalities of wealth and invidious distinctions of high and low. This is a great folly. In our arrogance we forget that we are all one day going to be levelled with the dust by death that knows no distinctions.
>
> — D.G. Tendulkar: *Mahatma,* Publications Division, Ministry of Information and Broadcasting, Government of India, 1969, Vol. VII, p. 212.

Admittedly, the vision of man *sans* any distinction of high and low, rich and poor, advantaged and disadvantaged is at the core of Gandhi's launching of the spinning-wheel. As a foreseer of humanity, he considers the spinning-wheel as a great messenger of the spirit of humanism to one and all. Lest he himself is misunderstood in his mission as above, he never fails to involve himself in the work of spinning regularly. It is a work that works challengingly in every sphere of life both inwardly and outwardly. It is a work that christens one with humane sensibilities like modesty, simplicity and austerity. It is also a work that conforms to the greatest Upanishadic vision of humanism for all time: *sarve sukhino bhavantu.* Let each of us be happy.

Gandhi advocates the humanistic spirit of the spinning-wheel primarily for four reasons. First, it allows creativity and freedom to work individually. Secondly, it synchronizes labour and love, and, as a consequence, bread labour becomes a natural reality. Thirdly, it harmonizes work with aesthetics. The beauty of creation by means of the spinning-wheel is not only an outward beauty catering to day-to-day necessities of life but also a beauty of inwardness. Such an inwardness heightens one to be in unison with one's Divine Self. Fourthly, it has a great unifying force that challenges all constraints of humanistic endeavour. Being an ardent and disciplined follower of the Gandhian essence of the spinning-wheel, one cannot but embrace the goodness of all.

A symbol of truth and non-violence as the spinning-wheel is, Gandhi advocates for each and every person in the pursuit of humanism to be loyal to it. The twofold purpose that he wants to be served by it is that it would bring about a change in everyone both inwardly and outwardly. Then the opponents would also be endeared and christened in the spinning-wheel promoting truth and non-violence. Highlighting this humanistic spirit of the spinning-wheel, he advises the *Satyagrahis:*

> I know that you will not fight unless you have me with you, but then you must know that I am here and I would fight only as a representative of those dumb millions for whom I live and for whom I want to die. My loyalty to them is greater than any other loyalty, and it is for them that I would not give up the *Charkha* even if you were to forsake me or kill me. *** The *Charkha* is an outward symbol of truth and non-violence, and unless you have them in your hearts you will not take to the *Charkha* either. Remember, therefore, that you have to fulfil both the internal and external conditions. If you fulfil the internal condition, you will cease to hate your opponent, you will not seek or work for his destruction, but pray to God to have mercy on him. Do not, therefore, concentrate on showing the misdeeds of the Government, for we have to convert and befriend those who run it. And, after all, no one is wicked by nature. And if others are wicked, are we the less so?
>
> — M.K. Gandhi: *Harijan,* 30 March, 1940.

When Gandhi highlights the spinning-wheel in terms of *Satyagraha* as above and accelerates the spirit of humanism, he teaches us the lesson of how to do justice to the inner soul in everyone of us. He advises us that material prosperity counts little for the inner soul, and therein lies the importance of the spinning-wheel to teach us the invaluable lesson of austerity. The lesson of humanity which is, indeed, the lesson of simplicity and serenity coupled with poignance and purity, leads to one's involvement in the spinning-wheel because the latter alone cares for the true spirit of *Satyagraha* and, therefore, of humanism. The quest for *Satyagraha* always incorporates the quest for inwardness, where the spinning-wheel plays a very significant role in learning and disseminating the lesson of humanism. Gandhi's own experimentation of harmonization of a global society on the principle of non-violence has its close association with the spinning-wheel which wages a relentless war against down-trodden humanity. As he poignantly observes:

> The accumulated experience of the past thirty years, the first eight of which were in South Africa, fills me with the greatest hope that in the adoption of non-violence lies the future of India and the world. It is the most harmless and yet equally effective way of dealing with the political and economic wrongs of the down-trodden portion of humanity. I have known from early youth that non-violence is not a cloistered virtue to be practised by the individual for peace and final salvation, but it is a rule of conduct for society if it is to live consistently with human dignity and makes progress towards the attainment of peace for which it has been yearning for ages past.
>
> —M.K. Gandhi: *Gandhiji's Correspondence with the Government, 1942-44,* Navajivan Publishing House, Ahmedabad, 1945, p. 170.

With *Charkha* as the embryonic humanistic force of non-violence Gandhi paves his unparalleled avenue of fighting against all odds either within or outside every human being. He looks upon it as sources of indomitable power to control the inner being so much so that the outward temptations hardly overpower it. Moreover the very engagement with the spinning-wheel makes one conscious of one's own power of forging ahead with untiring zeal against all opposing forces.

What Gandhi essentially desires through incorporation of the spinning-wheel in every home and in every society is to do away with narrowness of vision with regard to growth and development of humanism. It is neither a means of a fashionable enterprise nor an exposure of sentimentalism in the outward form of exercise of freedom as many persons even now assess it in utter misunderstanding. It is a means alive and dynamic for turning all oddities of life into a disciplined dynamic fervour of humanism.

A humanistic approach to education by means of introducing the spinning-wheel as Gandhi earnestly wants in *Nai Talim* or Basic Education, has at its backdrop the realistic story of appalling differences writ large in standards of living among the rural and the urban people. A positive approach to the revival of crafts and a special drive to introduce the spinning-wheel everywhere would not only revitalize economic harmony but also remove alienations among all sections of people in the villages and in the cities. Indeed, he wants to humanize education by vocationalizing it so that a good deal of harmonious relationship between man and man in rural and urban areas exists in reality, and, for this end-in-view, the spinning-wheel plays a pioneering role. As Gandhi unfolds his mission:

> Today our villages have become a mere appendage to the cities. They exist, as it were, to be exploited by the latter and depend on the latter's sufferance. This is unnatural. It is only when the cities realise the duty of making an adequate return to the villages for the strength and sustenance which they derive from them, that a healthy and moral relationship between the two will spring up. And if the city children are to play their part in this great and noble work of social reconstruction, the vocations through which they are to achieve their education ought to be directly related to the requirements of the villages. So far as I can see, the various processes of cotton manufacture from ginning and clearing of cotton to the spinning of yarn, answer this test as nothing else does. Even today cotton is grown in the villages and is ginned and spun and converted into cloth in the cities. But the chain of processes which cotton undergoes in the mills from the beginning to the end constitutes a huge tragedy of waste in men, materials and mechanical power.
>
> —M.K. Gandhi: *Harijan,* 9 October, 1937.

Revival of the sense of humanism by means of introducing the spinning-wheel amongst all sections of people as Gandhi earnestly desires, appears improbable not because it has in its inner vision the spirit of adventure that remains unknown to most of us, but essentially because we fight shy of endearing what is our very own. Rooted to our own inheritance and culture, it has its permanent appeal to each and everyone of us, but then, what fails to attract our attention in connection with the humanistic spirit of the spinning-wheel is that we never care to probe its deeper and finer role in bringing about a slow but sure and steady transformation first in our very approach to life and reality and then in our morbid and duped consciousness. It is, indeed, an irony that the lesson of humanism as put forward by the spinning-wheel which constitutes the essence of Gandhi's philosophy of work as worship, has yet remained unattended to by a schizophrenic humanity. Our children are now devoid of the music of the spinning-wheel which harmonizes the basic components of human development e.g. love, sympathy, co-operation, endurance and control of passion and sentimentalism. Being widely conversant and experienced with practical humanism.[1] Gandhi's concern with the spinning-wheel is directly and essentially participation of the common man for well-balanced and communicated living. Man as he earnestly feels must feel the woes and agonies of man wasted in the extravagance of bankruptcy in humanism. Let not the life of man be so cheap and negligible to be identified as abstractions or mere numbers or consumable goods in terms of mockeries of technocracy and sham affluence. Let the eternal spirit of the inner man—the man Divine and most beautiful—be nursled in the spirit of Truth which can be best cultivated in one's devotion to the spinning-wheel.

The *Brahmacharya* that Gandhi refers to in terms of humanism is actually the control of the mind by controlling the body. This requires an effective means which is best served by the spinning-wheel because it teaches how to control the mind by continuous and sustained devotion to physical labour through the spinning-wheel. A certain balanced approach to thought, word and deed essentially demands a disciplined approach to life and work where the spinning-wheel is not only a tool for physical exercise but for mental and spiritual exercise as well. It does not at any cost allow the mind to harbour impure thoughts. Therein lies observance of true *Brahmacharya* and, therefore, of true humanism. As Gandhi clearly spells out,

> *Brahmacharya* must be observed in thought, word and deed. It may be harmful to suppress the body, if the mind is at the same time allowed to go astray. When the mind wanders, the body must follow sooner or later.
>
> It is necessary here to appreciate a distinction. It is one thing to allow the mind to harbour impure thoughts, it is a different thing altogether if it strays among them in spite of ourselves. Victory will be ours in the end, if we non-co-operate with the mind in its evil wanderings.
>
> We experience every moment of our lives that often while the body is subject to our control, the mind is not. This physical control should never be relaxed, and in addition we must put forth a constant endeavour to bring the mind under control. We can do nothing more, nothing less.
>
> —M.K. Gandhi: *From Yeravda Mandir,* Navajivan Publishing House, Ahmedabad, 1935, p. 18.

Admittedly, the role of the spinning-wheel as the exponent of vibrant humanism demands a rethinking right now. It is an invaluable tool that paves path to better introspection and better involvement of the individual to prove his individual worth for march towards purity and perfection. The music of the spinning-wheel is, as it were, the life-blood for a revolution of consciousness for the ascent and excellence of man.

Plain living or living nobly as true humanism always aims at, is the *sine qua non* of the spinning-wheel. It is this essential component of humanism that is always at the backdrop of the philosophy of the spinning-wheel. This is why Gandhi's war against complicated material life begins with self-identification and self-respect, where the spinning-wheel is undeniably a very effective means to an end and never an end in itself.

Let all inhumanities exhibited in rampant spread of machinery and industrialization be challenged with humane sensitivities in exercising freedom of work with the spinning-wheel where creative endeavour is prized with the outcome enjoyed and appreciated in austerity and simplicity. Let high thinking be not crushed under the violence of Mammon worship gradually eating up the vitalities and 'grace of life'. The Gandhian forethoughts of humanism have their genesis on revival of 'simple but ennobled life' where the spinning-wheel plays the most significant role of revaluation of values. As Gandhi categorically remarks:

> I don't believe that industrialization is necessary in any case for any country. It is much less so for India. Indeed, I believe that independent India can only discharge her duty towards a groaning world by adopting a simple but ennobled life by developing her thousands of cottages and living at peace with the world. High thinking is inconsistent with complicated material life based on high speed imposed on us by Mammon worship. All the grace of life are possible only when we learn the art of living nobly.
>
> There may be sensation in living dangerously. We must draw the distinction between living in the face of danger and living dangerously. A man who dares to live alone in a forest infested by wild beasts and wilder men without a gun and with God as his only help, lives in the face of danger. A man who lives perpetually in mid-air and dives to the earth below to the admiration of a gaping world, lives dangerously. One is a purposeful, the other a purposeless life.
>
> Whether such plain living is possible for an isolated nation, however, large geographically and numerically, in the face of a world armed to the teeth and in the midst of pomp and circumstance,

is a question open to the doubt of a sceptic. The answer is straight and simple.

If plain life is worth living, then the attempt is worth making even though only an individual or a group makes the effort.

—D.G. Tendulkar: *Mahatma,* Publications Division, Ministry of Information and Broadcasting, Government of India, 1969, Vol. II, p. 188.

The philosophy of plain living and high thinking as Gandhi wants to introduce by means of the spinning-wheel has its distinct bearing upon remoulding national character. He despises idleness as it actually cripples the human mind and makes room for all evils that tarnish humanism. It is, indeed, a shame, as Gandhi reminds us again and again, to live as a parasite. It is also a shame as he draws our attention many times, to live a life of humiliation. Man must live with all his qualities of head and heart well exercised and manifested for the cause of humanism. He must live with all his identities expressed in terms of efflorescence of the soul. Hence, the importance of dissemination of the message of the spinning-wheel. His categorical advice is not to dehumanize man by alleviating poverty through charity:

Do not say you will maintain the poor on charity. Only two classes of people are entitled to charity and no one else—the *Brahmana* who possesses nothing and whose business it is to spread holy learning, and the cripple and the blind. The iniquitous system of giving doles to the able-bodied idle is going on to our eternal shame and humiliation, and it is to wipe out that shame that I am going about with the message of the *Charkha* up and down the whole country.

— M.K. Gandhi, *Young India,* 24 February, 1927.

Gandhi earnestly believes that the man of the heart awaits marriage of intellect and emotion which is real humanism. Such humanism finds its most fitting language in the music of the spinning-wheel. The emotion of man necessitates a discipline, a control, an adjustment, a routinized expression in the language of work turned into devotion and worship of the Divine Being in oneself. The spinning-wheel is that specific exponent of man allowing man to eliminate or transform and transcend emotion, as the case may be, and also steer him towards the eternal path of Truth, Beauty and Goodness. Gandhi's dream of an independent India is enkindled with the spirit of humanism derived from the spinning-wheel where the involvement of man as he categorically asserts, must be based on all seriousness of purpose:

> I cannot be satisfied, not till every man and woman in India is working at his or at her wheel. Burn that wheel if you find a better substitute. This is the one and only work which can supply the needs of the millions without disturbing them from their homes.
>
> After all, a lip-profession of faith in the *Charkha* and the throwing of a few rupees at me in a patronising manner won't bring *Swaraj* and won't solve the problem of the ever-deepening poverty of the toiling and starving millions, I want to correct myself. I have said toiling millions. I wish that it was a true description. Unfortunately, as we have not revised our tastes about clothing, we have made it impossible for these starving millions to toil throughout the year. We have imposed upon them a vacation, which they do not need, for at least four months in the year.
>
> — M.K. Gandhi, *Young India,* 15 September, 1927.

A symbol of 'commercial peace' as Gandhi eyes the spinning-wheel in terms of humanism it is more than a mere instrument for providing man with work and money. The inner vision with which it is blessed, is one of humanism which finds its manifestation in empathy in the midst of austerity and simplicity. The wheel with which one spins the yarn, also spins the essence of humanism. It carries within it the inroads to inner awakening. It spreads the message of love that purifies one in practice of perfection of humanism. And that perfection is a pointer to one's extinction of personality. Gandhi himself is an unparalleled illustration for ages to come:

> I am a poor mendicant. My earthly possessions consist of six spinning-wheel, prison dishes, a can of goat's milk, six home-spun loin-cloths and towels, and my reputation which cannot be worth much.
>
> —D.G. Tendulkar: *Mahatma,* Publications Division, Ministry of Information and Broadcasting, Government of India, 1962, Vol. III, p. 142.

With austerity and simplicity as the primal aspect of humanism well-exercised by means of the spinning-wheel, Gandhi wants to orient the life of man in the service of humanistic pursuit. There is always a certain sense of consciousness born of Truth and Goodness in particular, which, as he earnestly feels, should always be steered towards the excellence and ascent of mankind.

Gandhi's concept of humanism as reflected in the constructive programme of activities by means of the spinning-wheel is always geared to self-analysis through self-activity and self-appreciation. The involvement of every human being with the spinning-wheel is the prelude to the vision of the self from the point of view of altruism. Just as Gandhi involves the individual with the spirit of non-violence in the same way does he involve him or her with the spirit of the spinning-wheel. In both cases, the point of resemblance is that of extinction of self-interest and dissemination of the greater and the nobler interest: let all of us be attuned to the divine spirit of service for ascent of the self.

In the final analysis, Gandhi makes a serene fusion between humanism and spiritualism, between service to man and service to the All Excellent in man, by means of the inner music of the spinning-wheel. Therefore, it would be erroneous to narrow down this essential spirit of the spinning-wheel by highlighting its role in the struggle for freedom and social change. It would also be erroneous to consider it a mere tool for negotiating idleness and passivity. The music of the spinning-wheel, the swan song of humanism in the welfare of every human being is yet to be sung. Meanwhile, much more time is lost in its misassessment. Perhaps the muse ahead awaits a confession to be prized with the real vision of the All Serene through the spinning-wheel:

> The song that I came to sing remains unsung to this day.
> I have spent my days in stringing and in unstringing my instrument.
> The time has not come true, the words have not been rightly set; only there is the agony of wishing in my heart.
> The blossom has not opened: only the wind is sighing by.
> I have not seen his face, nor have I listened to his voice; only I have heard his gentle footsteps from the road before my house.
> The livelong day has passed in spreading his seat on the floor; but the lamp has not been lit and I cannot ask him into my house.
>
> — Rabindranath Tagore: *Gitanjali,* Macmillan India Limited, Macmillan Pocket Tagore Edition, 1983, No. XIII, pp. 8-9.

When would we attune ourselves with the inner spirit of the spinning-wheel?

NOTE

1. While discussing Gandhian humanism in terms of truth and non-violence, Professor S. Chakrabarti significantly remarks:

Ruskin's *Unto This Last,* which Gandhi read in 1904, denounced classical economists for not conceiving economics in terms of human welfare and accused industrialism of being responsible for intensifying poverty and injustice. These ideas found in a ready response in Gandhi's mind. The ideal of simple life and the stress on manual work took on their true significance in his quest. He found that though science and technology had given a new turn to the wheel of production and wealth, men were not only not emancipated, but were in fact being exploited. To Gandhi man himself was the cause of his own exploitation, because he had created machines and a huge centralised structure, and thus both in the political and economic fields, man had defeated man. He, therefore, called for a review of the old assumptions and for a reassessment of the scale of values. His emphasis on simplicity and limitation of wants, his stress on decentralisation and participation by the common man in the decision-making process at various levels, his call to men to work with joy, his emphasis on a united but not a uniform world—all this has a current relevance.

— S. Chakravarti: Truth and Non-Violence in Gandhi's Humanism', *Truth and Non-Violence,* T.K. Mahadevan (ed.), Gandhi Peace Foundation, New Delhi, 1970, p. 40.

7

POSTSCRIPT

'I CRAVE to die with my hand at the spinning-wheel', so ardently expresses Mahatma Gandhi. The craving of his soul has its genuine urge for love and humanism so endearing and yet so rare in a world of futility and frustration. With growing anxieties of a modern world destined to be at the mercy of nuclear warfare, the antidote to violence definitely lies in controlling passions and caressing serenity of the soul. The birth of man is itself an enigma and a promise of perfection, and the spinning-wheel is one that assures that promise with all simplicity and devotion guaranteed in its ends-in-view.

Today's man may think himself aloof from the beckoning of the soul harbouring in his own mind. He may also be far away from involving himself in any activity concerning the spinning-wheel. But that does not necessarily imply the absence of the humming sound of the spinning-wheel from his own action and contemplation. Rather does he seek the avenue of emancipation from the dragonland of utilitarianism. This has its outward manifestation writ large in the society. A certain sense of dissipation coupled with that of satiety not only embarks upon a stuffed man of the modern world, 'headpiece filled with straw' but also engulfs the vision of the spinning-wheel so much so that we do want to seek solace and contentment by means of self-involvement in the spinning-wheel.

Apart from the fact that the modern man is a victim to sham modernity, Gandhi as a foreseer of debunking humanism, hammers the truth of returning to the roots of self-excellence by means of self-involvement and self-devotion. Hence, the importance of the spinning-wheel in the life and philosophy of man.

The inherent purpose of the spinning-wheel in terms of the Gandhian philosophy of man as indicated above is to allow man to be 'men' and *vice-versa.* Therefore, Gandhi wants to emphasize it as the focal point of the ascent of man and society. It cannot but go deep into the hearts of millions of men in diverse walks of life. It cannot but penetrate into the everyday affairs of every human being. The music it offers cannot but be the music arising out of the harmony and peace of the entire human society.

The spinning-wheel, indeed, voices the vision of Gandhi from fourfold avenue. First, it makes everyone aware of his own position in the society. Second, it brings forth a spirit of activity intrinsic as well as extrinsic. Third, it allows everyone to assess himself in terms of his involvement with it under trying circumstances. Fourth, it instils a spirit of marching ahead with further aspirations of the discovery of the human hearts under diverse human habitations.

Gandhi also visualizes the harmony of the human soul not in religiosity but in the socio-spiritual involvement of man through the spinning-wheel. Why does he choose it for this purpose or end-in-view? His own interpretation of the spinning-wheel as the 'only' religion refers to the fact that the emancipation of man and society so ardently desired, awaits work ennobled as worship. Gandhi teaches the new lesson of religion of man by means of the spinning-wheel that does away with religiosity and allows everyone to be justified to himself by devotion to exercise of functional religion. The strategy he adopts is simple and clear, appealing and soul-stirring, for the spinning-wheel has some extra-ordinary power when handled with all seriousness of purpose to prove that:

(a) It is a non-violent means of devotion to work for self-contentment and self-dependence.
(b) It caters to the needs of the individual as well as society.
(c) It ensures realization of the indigenous power of self-growth and self-development.
(d) It allows a newer approach to honour one's own religion of work and saves one from being a pawn to alien resources.
(e) It gives a new dimension to the thinktanks of an individual and the nation.

For an emergence of an altruistic society, Gandhi looks upon the spinning-wheel not merely an instrument to negotiate idle time but, more than anyone else, also to go beyond time and needs as these pose towards humanity in manifold ways. His concerns is dynamic socialism with which everyone should be provided and allowed to prosper. Therefore, the music of the spinning-wheel is one of dynamism vibrant with the fulfilment of the Upanisadic saying *Charaiveti*—march ahead.

Gandhi also crystallizes the dynamic spirit derived from the spinning-wheel by embracing the whole society irrespective of caste, creed, community, race, religion or status whatsoever. This inevitably encompasses the spirit of living together and living whole-heartedly for the well-being of one and all. This is why the spinning-wheel narrows down social disparities and makes a favourable ground to boost a more or less balanced economy with its primary objective of eliminating horrible differences between man and man. This is equally true in the context of social ukase at present. Hence, the importance of the Gandhian philosophy of the spinning-wheel in both theory and practice.

The Gandhian concept of the spinning-wheel as an incomparable instrument of socio-economic synchronization has a special appeal because it is broad-based and above bias towards a particular section of the society—a fact, very often ignored and ill-treated. Indeed, the role of the spinning-wheel is surprisingly underrated even now because there is an appalling ignorance well-bred in the misconcept that it is just to appease the socially ostracized. Gandhi never steers the spinning-wheel towards any vested and impure interest, nor does he ever think of introducing it as a mere patch-up strategy for alleviating poverty. Deep in his heart of hearts is the muse of the glory of man and this music, if well-exercised by means of endearing the spinning-wheel, can be a permanent source of glorifying the dignity of man.

Gandhi wants to change the very attitude of man towards man and society and *vice-versa* by introducing the spinning-wheel. He strongly believes and actually proves it in performance that it generates a certain sense of fearlessness which is very essential for development of personality. This fearlessness is also closely related to the exercise of freedom. Unfortunately, the spinning-wheel is dishonoured in merely considering it an exercise of freedom for the sake of freedom. Gandhi never drags it down to some apparent gain in the form of so-called exercise of freedom. Freedom of the mind as well as of the heart is the fundamental point of interest, which, when derived through the spinning-wheel, becomes more dynamic, more psychological, more effective for orientation of human behavioural designs, specially the attitude towards it. It becomes more vocal and more endearing than exercise of brute force, for example, because its backdrop is all the time guided by the music of the spinning-wheel that teaches the lesson of discipline so badly necessary for its appropriate role.

The lesson that Gandhi wants to disseminate by means of the spinning-wheel is inward discipline so important for the training of the minds as well as of the spirit inherent in man. He believes that outward discipline has very little to do for regeneration of man. This is why he fights shy of physical force and concentrates entirely on the mental and spiritual force. The mind of man as he more than once claims, is more powerful than his body. The spinning-wheel is the surest means of exercise of the mind of man where physical exercise is relegated to the background. This more clearly explains that its primary concern is not to retaliate the idleness of man as such but the idleness of his mind which, if not well arrested in time, eats up and destroys his inherent vitality.

Gandhi does not care for physical growth so much so that it comes at crossroads with mental growth. On the other hand, the role of man in accelerating mental growth somehow or other teaches the lesson to himself that it often negates the former as redundant. This is typically true with respect to the Indian concept of growth in man, where growth might direct towards spiritual growth where physical growth becomes a blob. Otherwise, extinction of the physical self in the forms of denial and disapproval of food, drink and so on would have become a myth. Who denies the stout physique of almost every devout Indian hermit living on inhaling and exhaling air for months together? Gandhi himself proves, through his observance of fasting, that man lives by inward discipline and this can be well-exercised by control of body, mind and spirit, where the spinning-wheel becomes one of the most powerful component of such human endeavour. The discipline that one undergoes through it becomes a means to an end, that is perfection from every possible aspect of manifestation of personality and never an end in itself. It is neither a tool nor a force with which one should be overburdened as it is very often assumed but a promising symbol of stick-to-itiveness to Truth, Goodness and Beauty.

Admittedly, Gandhi makes a significant departure from embankment of humanism upon utilitarianism which is at present a sordid commentary of human life. He welcomes the spinning-wheel in our day-to-day life as it teaches the lessons of aesthetics in the most practical way. The loin cloth—a direct product of the spinning-wheel—represents simplicity, modesty, austerity and contentment which are the definite components of Beauty and Goodness. when one whole-heartedly accepts the loin cloth as the product of the spinning-wheel he also endears the aesthetic components as above and translates these components in practical life into a living force for advancement of humanism.

The harbouring of the human spirit upon aesthetics in practical life so important for cultivation of inward discipline is also harbouring of the human spirit upon aesthetic sensibilities. There is no room for emotional instability, for the outcome of emotion very often betrays advancements of personality. The spirit that Gandhi wants to be geared up through the spinning-wheel is one of devotion born out of discipline and absence of unwanted display of emotion.

The philosophy of the spinning-wheel that Gandhi wants to assert by introducing it as an ideal means for nursling inward discipline is always based on the aesthetics of love. He spurns a doled-out life like a parasite and, instead, adorns the life of action well steered by mutual love and cooperation. The love that one learns by exercise of the spinning-wheel is always one pure and appealing, unalloyed and pleasing. It is born out of simplicity and is also rooted to one's natural atmosphere. It, therefore, remains far from being alien for a single moment in course of one's involvement with it from time immemorial. The yarn that one spins by means of it, is one that pulsates the development of one's having, loving and being at the same time and in the most spontaneous way. When Gandhi identifies it as the living symbol of humanism, the truth that emerges is the warmth of the aesthetic spirit of love and sympathy which serves as an abiding force in the ascent of man and society.

Side by side with the exercise of the aesthetic spirit of love, Gandhi also wants to incorporate the spirit of forbearance which forms an indispensable part of inward discipline. As a foreseer of humanism, he advocates the spinning-wheel which binds the two vital forces of human development viz., love and forbearance. While his principle of non-violence acts as a theoretical force, the spinning-wheel serves the practical one. Its humming sound goes deep into the hearts of millions of people who by forgetting hatred and impatience sing the swan song of communicated and harmonious living.

Gandhi also bases his spinning-wheel on the platform of culture and civilization. If culture stands for advanced development of the human powers and civilization for harmonious human relationships, the spinning-wheel serves as the ideal exponent for both. Gandhi wants to advocate a new culture and civilization through it for it always remains above suspicion and corruption whatsoever. As it believes in unwarranted exposure of the person involved, it leaves no room for ambiguity. It has an appeal both to the head and to the heart, and as such, it makes a marriage of the person in intellect and the same in emotion. Gandhi incomparably makes an eternal inroad to exercise of the inward excellence of man by means of the spinning-wheel. In fact, the basic intention of his launching of the spinning-wheel is to allow everyone devoted to it to adjust himself most appropriately in the fine and delicate balance of intellect and emotion. It is rather an irony in the post-Gandhian era of human development that that very crucial experiment. of making a well-balanced fusion between intellect and emotion has been relegated to the background, leaving aside the spinning-wheel, the wheel of the dynamic humanism, in the world of oblivion.

Nevertheless, if today's man is the representative of the man of tomorrow or day after tomorrow, he cannot but owe his allegiance to finer visions and truths of the past. The Gandhian philosophy of the spinning-wheel becomes all the more prominent with reference to the above as it caters to whatever is true, good and beautiful, and whatever leads man to the march of fulness of personality. The thread coming out of the spinning-wheel is the eternal thread of well-embracing humanity.

Meanwhile, let us pray to the All Beautiful to be justified to Him through our actions:

> Life of my life, I shall ever try to keep my body pure,
> knowing that thy living touch is upon all my limbs.
>
> I shall ever try to keep all untruths out from my thoughts,
> knowing that thou art that truth which has kindled the
> light of reason in my mind.
>
> I shall ever try to drive all evils away from my heart and
> keep my love in flower, knowing that thou hast thy seat
> in the inmost shrine of my heart.
>
> And it shall be my endeavour to reveal thee in my actions
> knowing it is thy power gives me strength to act.
>
> — Rabindranath Tagore: *Gitanjali,* Macmillan India Limited, Macmillan Pocket, Tagore Edition, 1983, No. IV, p. 3.

BIBLIOGRAPHY

Andrews, C.F., *Mahatma Gandhi at Work,* Macmillan, London, 1931

Ashe, Geoffrey, *Gandhi, A Study in Revolution,* Stain & Day, New York, 1968.

Bharathi, K.S., *The Social Philosophy of Mahatma Gandhi,* Concept Publishing Company, New Delhi, 1991.

Bhattacharya, Buddhadeva, *Evolution of the Political Philosophy of Gandhi,* Calcutta Book House, Calcutta, 1969.

Bondurant, John, *Conquest of Violence,* Princeton University, 1958.

Bose, N.K., *My Days with Gandhi,* Nishana, Calcutta, 1953.

Catlin, George, *In the Path of Mahatma Gandhi,* Macdonald & Co., London, 1948.

Chakrabarti, Mohit, *Gandhian Mysticism,* Atlantic Publishers and Distributors, New Delhi, 1989.

—, *The Gandhian Dimensions of Education,* Daya Publishing House, Delhi, 1990.

—, *Gandhian Aesthetics,* Atlantic Publishers and Distributors, New Delhi, 1990.

—, *Gandhian Humanism,* Concept Publishing Company, New Delhi, 1992.

—, *Gandhian Spiritualism,* Concept Publishing Company, New Delhi, 1993.

—, *Mahatma Gandhi: A Revaluation,* Ashish Publishing House, New Delhi, 1994.

—, *Gandhian Religion,* Gyan Publishing House, New Delhi, 1994.

—, *The Gandhian Philosophy of Man,* Harpercollins Publishers India Pvt. Ltd., New Delhi, 1995.

—, *Gandhian Socio-Aesthetics,* M.D. Publications Pvt. Ltd., New Delhi, 1997.

Desai, Mahadev, *Gandhiji in Indian Villages,* S. Ganesan, Madras, 1927.

Diwakar, R.R., *Gandhi, The Spiritual Seeker,* Bharatiya Vidya Bhavan, Bombay, 1964.

Easwaran, Eknath, *Gandhi The Man,* Turnston Press, Northumptonshire, U.K., 1983.

Erikson, Erik H., *Gandhi's Truth,* Norton & Company, New York, 1969.

Fischer, Louis, (ed.) *The Essential Gandhi,* George Allen & Unwin Ltd., London, 1963.

Fulop-Miller, R., *Lenin and Gandhi,* F.S. Flint & D.F. Tait (Translated), Putnam, London.

Gandhi, M.K., *From Yeravda Mandir,* Navajivan Publishing House, Ahmedabad, 1935.

—, *Gandhiji's Correspondence with the Government,* Navajivan Publishing House, Ahmedabad, 1945.

—, *Speeches and Writings of Mahatma Gandhi,* G.A. Natesan & Company, Madras, 1934.

—, *Swaraj Through Charkha,* All India Spinners' Association, Sevagram, 1945.

—, *Harijan.*

—, *Young India.*

—, *Gandhi Marg,* Journal of the Gandhi Peace Foundation, New Delhi.

Gangrade, K.D. & Misra, R.P., *Conflict Resolution Through Non-violence: Role of the Universities.* Vols. I-II, Concept Publishing Company, New Delhi.

Greg, Richard, *The Power of Non-Violence,* Schocken Books, New York, 1970.

Jack, Homer A., *Gandhi Reader,* Indiana University Press, U.S.A., 1962.

Mahadevan, T.K. (Ed.), *Truth and Non-Violence,* Gandhi Peace Foundation, New Delhi, 1970.

Nanda, B.R., *Mahatma Gandhi,* Beacon Press, Boston, 1958.

Payne, Robert, *The Life and Death of Mahatma Gandhi,* Bodley Head, London, 1969.

Prabhu, R.K. & Rao, U.R. (Compiled): *The Mind of Mahatma Gandhi,* Oxford University Press, London, 1945.

Pyarelal, *Mahatma Gandhi: The Last Phase,* Navajivan Publishing House, Ahmedabad, 1965.

Radhakrishnan, S., (ed.) *Mahatma Gandhi: Essays and Reflections,* Jaico, Bombay, 1956

Shean, Vincent, *Lead, Kindly Light,* Random House, New York, 1949.

Tagore, Rabindranath: *Gitanjali,* Macmillan India Limited, New Delhi, 1983.

Tendulkar, D.G.: *Mahatma,* Publications Division, Government of India, Vols. I-VIII.

Watson, F. & Brown, M., *Talking of Gandhiji,* Orient Longmans, Calcutta, 1957.

INDEX